D0344792

Female Identity Conflict in Clinical Practice

Female Identity Conflict in Clinical Practice

by Doris Bernstein

Norbert Freedman and Betsy Distler,
editors

with an Introduction by
Christopher Bollas

IPTAR Monograph Number Two

JASON ARONSON INC.
Northvale, New Jersey
London

Production Editor: Judith D. Cohen

This book was set in 12 point English Times by Lind Graphics of Upper Saddle River, New Jersey, and printed and bound by Haddon Craftsmen of Scranton, Pennsylvania.

Library of Congress Cataloging-in-Publication Data

Bernstein, Doris, 1932–1990.
    Female identity conflict in clinical practice / by Doris Bernstein
    Norbert Freedman and Betsy Distler, editors : with an introduction
by Christopher Bollas.
        p. cm.
    Includes bibliographical references and index.
    ISBN 0-87668-502-5 (hard cover)
    1. Women—Psychology. 2. Identity (Psychology) 3. Women and
psychoanalysis. 4. Psychosexual development. I. Freedman,
Norbert. II. Distler, Betsy. III. Title.
    [DNLM: 1. Gender Identity. 2. Oedipus Complex. 3. Superego.
4. Women—psychology. WM 460.5.I4 B531f]
RC451.4.W6B475 1993
155.3′33—dc20
DNLM/DLC
for Library of Congress   92-48974

Manufactured in the United States of America. Jason Aronson Inc. offers books and cassettes. For information and catalog write to Jason Aronson Inc., 230 Livingston Street, Northvale, New Jersey 07647.

Contents

Preface

With the publication of this book, we are officially ushering in Volume Two of the IPTAR Monograph Series. Like its predecessor, *Dream Portrait: A Study of Nineteen Sequential Dreams as Indicators of Pretermination,* by A. Bond, D. Franco, and A. K. Richards, it is a product of The Institute for Psychoanalytic Training and Research (IPTAR).

It seems appropriate at this point to say a word about IPTAR. IPTAR is a pioneering organization in the history of psychoanalysis in the United States. It was formed in 1958 in response to two trends: on the one hand, the widening interest in Freud and psychoanalysis that had been stimulated by the arrival in this country of outstanding European psychoanalysts; and on the other, the then prevalent restrictive training policies. Founded as an organization uniquely and consistently dedicated to classical psychoanalysis, it first provided a congenial setting for the exchange of ideas; soon afterward, it began to offer rigorous and thorough training in classical theory and technique for qualified students from a variety of academic and professional backgrounds. IPTAR continues today as an institute and society that has achieved a unique integration of the original Freudian text with the important elaborations and transformations of those original concepts that have led to the expanded understanding of psychopathology, development, technique, and application.

This volume is written and edited by IPTAR members, and most of its chapters originated as lectures at IPTAR public meetings, panel presentations, and workshops. Aside from their intrinsic value, these papers contributed greatly to the scientific life of our organization and to the ongoing psychoanalytic education of our members, thus meeting the criteria for inclusion in the IPTAR Monograph Series.

The editors, Norbert Freedman, three times IPTAR president as well as a Fellow, and Betsy Distler, IPTAR graduate and a Fellow, worked very closely with Doris Bernstein and are eminently qualified for the editing and integrative task they undertook. The introduction by our esteemed honorary member Christopher Bollas adds richness and sparkle to this volume. But above all we take pride in the fact that Doris Bernstein was a product of IPTAR, having graduated from our Training Institute. She also had the distinction of being the first graduate elected as IPTAR president, attesting to the respect in which she was held.

Daisy Franco
Publications Chairperson and
Editor, IPTAR Monograph Series

Portrait of an Analyst: Doris Bernstein (1932–1990)

The essays that appear in this volume, written in the last ten years of Doris Bernstein's life, represent the crystallization of her psychoanalytic thinking over three decades. They constitute a systematic exposition of her commitment to the concept of a gender-specific view of the clinical process. When she began to write these papers, she was already known as a revered teacher of clinical process and clinical theory and as a significant supervisor of psychoanalysis in the New York community.

Doris Bernstein was among the first graduates of The Institute for Psychoanalytic Training and Research (IPTAR). In quick succession, she joined the IPTAR faculty, became a training analyst, was twice elected to the presidency, and together with one of us, Norbert Freedman, was instrumental in leading IPTAR to become the first interdisciplinary psychoanalytic society in the United States to be accepted into the International Psychoanalytical Association, after many years of exclusion. She died shortly thereafter.

Doris Bernstein had her professional roots in classical psychoanalytic training; balanced against this was her identity as a professional woman seeking to find — or define — her place. Her thinking and career represent a continuing effort to synthesize these two commitments.

Before moving on to the substance of her work, we wish to pause to offer a sketch of Doris, our beloved friend and colleague.

This is a story of a very ordinary life in an extraordinary woman. Ordinary, in that it is the evolution of a bright professional woman finding her place in the decades of the '60s, '70s, and '80s. Ordinary, in that she was articulating the newly won consciousness of womanhood and the newly attained achievements of professional effectiveness. But within this frame we find the events of daily living processed in uncanny ways, creating new insights and new achievements. Let us sample some typical moments.

We see a woman going through the ordinary, repeated experience of sitting at the playground. It suddenly strikes her that she is so-and-so's mommy, so-and-so's daughter, so-and-so's wife: but who is she? Who is the woman, independent of the relationships in which she is embedded? And she begins to look at that. She hears it in her patients. When she does, it resonates within her. She takes it a step further: she puts it down on paper and shapes it into a statement. She has used it as a springboard to fight her way out of it, into a conceptualization of her own identity, that independent identity that drives the interpretive line in her analytic work, toward a crystallization of her patients' identity.

We see her at the library, another ordinary situation. She reads the classics — Oedipus, Antigone, Electra. Again, suddenly a connection, here not just to her patients' material but to psychoanalytic theory — theory of the nineteenth century and of the twentieth – and she is able to make an important conceptual shift. Is Electra a female Oedipus, or is there a difference? "I believe I have something to say." And here we have the genesis of the oedipal paper. What strikes her in working with the myths and trying to see what is relevant for women is the basic fact that Oedipus was a boy. A boy's body. It doesn't work, because a girl's body is different. What do we have to do to conceptualize something female, not not-male? Here she is moving from literature to the body to patients to contemporary theory, always restlessly trying to make connections.

We see her at a professional meeting, with its usual aura, a confluence of excitement, anxiety, and inevitable competitiveness. We see her listening to a critique of her own paper, a critique that was sometimes complimentary and sometimes condescending and even dismissive. She whispers to one of us, "I shall not be trivialized." This may be a statement of rage. It certainly is a statement of indignation. But in her mind it became rage transformed. She took one of us aside. "Let's go for a drink. I must not let my rage color all perception of maleness. If I'm simply enraged and feel injured, I will get nowhere." Later, she reflected, "That's why I'm concerned not just with the psychology of the female but with a gender-specific understanding of men as well."

We see a woman continuing to preserve the vitality of her body at all costs, even in the face of her progressing illness. Disregarding pain, she continues swimming thirty-eight laps a day, continues walking, continues to preserve the sense of physical aliveness in her body. When she is no longer able to swim, she continues to tend her terrace garden. She nourishes herself with her plants, a mutually nurturing world, the world of her childhood, one that speaks directly to her and connects her to her friends. It sustains her until the very end.

Finally, we see her negotiating the path of IPTAR as the first nonmedical institute accredited by the International Psychoanalytical Association, steering the course through the most turbulent of waters. She is a tough negotiator when the integrity of the Institute is threatened. Listening, waiting patiently, she then jells an unruly Board into coherent and consolidated action. A hostess, charming, yet unyielding at pivotal points of negotiation, she gives support and stability at moments when the task seems to be at the brink of failure. Then she reaps the fruits of all that effort: very much in pain, crippled, she travels to Rome and joins her colleagues to hear the ovation of 2,000 IPA delegates only a few months before her death.

After her death, the Doris Bernstein Section on the Study of Gender was created by the Board of Directors of IPTAR. Carrying on her work, this group of colleagues shaped a course on the psychoanalytic study of gender, established a study group and a scholarship, and continues to plan annual meetings and conferences. Doris lives on within us.

Norbert Freedman and Betsy Distler

Introduction

Christopher Bollas

Readers of much contemporary psychoanalytical literature will encounter views of the evolution of the self that incant now familiar and important concepts, such as the selfobject, the transitional object, or the notion of absence, of inscription, or of the imaginary, among many others. As psychoanalysis moves toward the centenary of the *Interpretation of Dreams* its theory is alive with the language of object relations and the desires of the subject, with many people rightfully celebrating the great post-Freudians: Klein, Kohut, Winnicott, and Lacan.

Although Doris Bernstein is more than conversant with the contemporary analytical literature, there is something wonderfully "of old" about her writing, which she rather announces by asserting early on that the reader needs to be reminded that Freud's two great works were the dream book and the monograph on infantile sexuality. How ironic, however, that what appears initially like something from the past should appear on the present scene in a burst of return, and in so doing, gather to itself that revolutionary quality that pervaded so much of Freud's work.

Bernstein's genius in this all-too-short monograph is to boldly return the human body to the center of psychoanalytic consideration. Ostensibly it is a book about the female identity and no reader will be let down on this score. Indeed, her profound examinations of the regressive effects of early female genital sensations, of how this gives a female character to the superego, and of how the young girl and the adult analysand use apparent regressive returns to earlier libidinal stages in order to experience a sense of mastery — a step back in order to move forward — puts this monograph in a class of its own. I simply have not read another psychoanalytical text that so exquisitely explores the psychical life of women.

But Bernstein's papers serve us in another important way, as she craftily insists that Freud's theory of the body ego implicitly demanded our consideration of such an ego in sexual terms. With this as a kind of point of embarkation, she rethinks the male and the female body, exploring how, in particular, the separate genital senses of the two sexes inform the body ego and how this in turn establishes a different psychical character for each sex. Her continuous links between bodily sensations, psychic outcomes, identity configurations, and the relations to the mother and the father weave a revitalized meaning into our considerations of subjectivity and intersubjectivity precisely because Doris Bernstein is unmatched as an analytical writer in her capacity to reembody psychoanalysis.

One must also admire and acknowledge the way she solves the "problem of instincts," insofar as in her hands instincts are given a clearly meaningful place in the psychoanalytic consideration of how the life of the body establishes its own psychic reality and how, in turn, this affects sexual identity and object relations. If instinct theory has suffered the ironic effect of being antiseptically considered in the somewhat anesthetized models of metapsychology, it roars back boldly in Bernstein's placement of instinct within the bodies of the developing girl and the growing boy. The gravest lack in contemporary psychoanalytic writings must be the underrepresentation of the instincts, bringing us to the brink of a psychoanalysis so denuded of the body that Freud's great feat of linkage — of body to and with mind — is on the verge of extinction. Yet I say, where Id was, in the literature of psychoanalysis, let works like those of Bernstein be. It is through the reading of this kind of literature that psychoanalytical candidates will be able to see the sense in instinct theory and in the vital role of the body in the life of the mind.

Bernstein's papers are written in a clear and concise prose. She uses psychoanalytical jargon sparingly but not to the point of negative hallucination; indeed, old terms come alive in her rethinking and recontextualizations of them. She is also direct and critical of other points of view, but never in a contentious way. It is helpful to see whom she disagrees with and precisely why. Above all else, however, is the voice of a passionate clinician, by which I mean the utterance of an obviously gifted clinician who cares deeply about her patients — in particular her female analysands — who could unnecessarily suffer at the hands of well-meaning psychoanalysts for lack of an adequate knowledge of female sexual identity. One can sense, then, that in writing about profoundly thought-provoking interpretations to her patients — ones that like Winnicott remarkably discover the generative move in the seemingly pathologic retreat — Bernstein is directly addressing her colleagues who fail to see that there is something intrinsic to female sexual identity that almost always uses temporary regressive routes to fashion the progressive articulation of the self.

Here then is a monograph that will teach everyone something that they thought they knew, but, upon reading, will discover, through a subtle yet insistently intelligent reviewing, that they did not know so well. It is a work that harks back to the beginnings of psychoanalysis and that recasts early theories of infantile sexuality and human identity in a language that is true to the body, but it is not cast in psychoanalytical models that will send readers into meandering daydreams. A riveting and compelling book that will, I am sure, be read for many generations to come, it arrives just in time and must surely be one of the early voices for the reclamation of the body in psychoanalysis. For this we are of course indebted to the author, but so too to the editors, Norbert Freedman and Betsy Distler, who have arranged the papers in a skillful order and provided helpful (and unobtrusive) notes to give the reader an increased sense of the place of any one essay in Bernstein's life.

1

Gender-Specific Attribution of Identity

Doris Bernstein and Norbert Freedman

Gender pervades every aspect of mental functioning. The ensuing pages will indicate the extent to which gender, as a mental construct, impinges upon those components of mental functioning that are pivotal to a psychoanalytic understanding of personality, whether the nature of unconscious phantasy, the organization of mental structures (superego and id), the organization of anxieties, the clinical process, or — and perhaps more fundamentally — our understanding of the epigenesis of mental life.

This very notion of the shaping role of gender in the development of psychic organization is deeply rooted in the writings of Freud. It is perhaps a sine qua non of a Freudian understanding of mental life. The two great Freudian discoveries of the turn of the century, which have survived the test of time, are the delineation of the reality of the unconscious (in *The Interpretation of Dreams*) and the notion of epigenetic development in boys and girls (in *Three Essays on the Theory of Sexuality*). The Freudian vision would not have survived without the concept of the dynamic unconscious and the notion of infantile sexuality. In each of these contributions, as well as in later ones (notably "Some Psychical Consequences of the Anatomical Distinction between the Sexes"), Freud has argued that gender is not simply a matter of social role, but rather, that the bodies into which we are born continue to permeate our lives.

And yet, Freud has articulated only half the equation. In emphasizing the shaping role of anatomy, Freud consistently used the male to construct his model. Let us remind ourselves that Oedipus was a little boy. While Freud did acknowledge that anatomy is destiny, in *his* brand of gender-specificity, he utilized the male model as the baseline and then defined the female as a deviation. Moreover, in his account of the treatment process, there tended to be the model of the male analyst facing the female patient. This is notably clear in his 1915 paper "Observations on Transference Love," where, in one memorable passage, he recommends that the patient overcome by erotic love be fed "soup and dumplings." The main intent in the ensuing pages of this book is to correct this imbalance. A vision will be delineated of the young girl, the growing woman, the female patient together with a female analyst, all within the framework of the psychoanalytic understanding of personality. But more generally, the emphasis is not simply on the female or on the male, but on a gender-specific view of mental development.

The issue of the specificity of an organizing identity linked to gender is given powerful expression in the consideration of a castration complex as it emerges in both boys and girls. When Freud used the term *genital anxiety,* he really meant castration anxiety; to this he attributed the same force, the same psychic impact in the girl—who may indeed have the phantasy of having a penis—as he did the phantasy based upon a biological reality in the boy. If one adheres to Freud's assumption of the importance of anatomy in mental representations, then anatomical differences do, in fact, play an important role: a "phantasy organ" could not have nearly the same psychic reality in the process of phantasy construction as does a real organ. This discrimination is a very important one. The fallacy here is that in the case of the female, the attribution of identity is founded not on what she has, but on what she does *not* have. The defining characteristics of her own genitals are not even under consideration in discussions of the shaping of her body ego.

These considerations allow us to approach a notion of gender specificity. Such a notion must be based on the positive and identifiable attributes of gender in each of the sexes. It rests thus not on absence but on presence. Since so much has been written on the presence in the case of the male, the corrective is, of necessity, the presence of identifiable attributes that form the foundation of the representational world in the female. In most general terms, gender specificity is framed, or prefigured, by the biological or physiological givens in the developmental process in males and females, and in the process in which they undergo repression or reappear in circuitous ways throughout the life cycle.

DEVELOPMENTAL CONSIDERATIONS IN GENDER SPECIFICITY

Having delineated a general position of gender-specific identity, it behooves us to distinguish this perspective from those commentaries in the literature that negate or deemphasize early gender differentiation. We are referring here to contributions since Jones and Horney, who were the pioneers in the critique of the Freudian text — or, to put it

another way, Freud's abuse of the female psyche. Over the
past three or four decades, that early criticism has been
accepted. What has ensued since are various efforts that
nonetheless fail to recognize the specific biological sources
underlying mental functioning and its specificity in the
developing female. (This does not include the empirical
literature on child observation, but the analytic literature.)
For instance, the literature on early object relations (Winnicott, Fairbairn) emphasizes that we all come from the same
source (our mothers), that we have the same anxieties about
being alone, about communicating or not communicating,
about distinguishing the me from the not-me, and so on.
Gender-related roles that develop later are grafted onto the
earliest experiences (this is true in Kleinian theory as well).
This flies against the fact that the little girl experiences her
body differently, from the earliest phases of being. It flies
against the facts of research findings, where early gender
differences have been documented, and against the retro-
spective constructions encountered in clinical practice. And
yet the mythology of a unisex development persists, despite
the fact that the basic equipment is different.

Among the plethora of contemporary contributions to a
psychodynamic vision of gender development, the work of
Irene Fast (cf. 1979) deserves mention. Her work has a
twofold aspect: on the one hand, it escapes the view that the
little girl inevitably faces castration, that is, is confronted
with the inescapable fate of a depressive experience. Instead,
Fast bases her view on a theory of narcissism and bisexuality.
Since narcissism inevitably includes a desire to encompass
everything, the me and the not-me, the desired object and the
eschewed object, it must also include the desire to encompass
the attributes of both sexes. If the presence of bisexual
strivings is granted from the earliest beginning, then bisexual
strivings are an inevitable by-product of a narcissistic state of
consciousness. Gender differentiation implies the willingness

to relinquish a bisexual mode of experiencing. This is a satisfactory account for the early process of differentiation;
however, it fails to account for an intrinsic genital striving. A
gender-specific view would hold that differentiation is im-
pelled by the desire to pursue intrinsically male or female
goals.

Thus far, emphasis has been on pregenital identity and its
disregard. A Freudian understanding asserts, of course, that
gender has a developmental progression, hence the pivotal
role of the genital phase. It is a central thesis that in both the
boy and the girl, genitality, achieved in the third year of life,
has a distinct organizing function. Genitality signifies a new
sense of autonomy. It is one thing to achieve autonomy
through separation from the mother, that is, dyadic autonomy; it is another to feel autonomous in a triangular setting,
experiencing both one's attachment, sameness, and identity
with one's mother, *and* one's separateness. As will be seen,
this has profound implications for superego development
and for the playing out of the oedipal situation. Genitality as
a positive developmental event on the pathway to autonomy
in the female has been neglected in analytic theory. If the
image of the girl's identity is described simply as the absence
of these organizing traits, she winds up with a pregenital
character (one of the critiques of the women's movement).
This psychoanalytic understanding, based on identifiable,
bodily rooted strivings toward autonomy in the growing girl,
creates a vision of women's identity. After all, if only the
phallic principle is considered as the primary psychic organizer, then autonomy is circumscribed to an experience of
male sexuality in men and women alike.

PERSPECTIVES ON ANXIETY

An ordinary notebook of process recording of the analytic
material of our female patients cannot help but convince us

how profoundly the woman's experience of her body shapes the mental representations. This is certainly also true in the shaping of anxieties. A typical dream has a house with windows all around — "I am worried about getting locks, it's so open" — or a building in which the woman is anxiously trying to secure the doors and windows, barring entry. These may be allusions to a fear of invasion and a fear of genital entry. There are other forms of specifically female genital anxieties as well, having to do with access and diffusivity. They all demonstrate the overriding importance of the woman's experience, often unconscious, of her body. This may delineate the content of the anxieties and point to the pattern of defensive layering, the modes of mastery and control.

Freud has provided a framework for the understanding of anxiety. His second theory of anxiety (1926) has received wide acceptance, even in nonpsychoanalytic quarters. Here he emphasizes the signal and anticipatory function of anxiety, and here also he provides a developmental frame for the understanding of anxiety, from annihilation anxiety, to separation anxiety, to castration anxiety, and finally to guilt anxiety. Overriding this conception is not only the idea that there are developmentally specific forms of anxiety but also the notion that when anxiety functions as a signal, there exist situations of danger to the integrity of the organism or the self. These danger situations are defined by the notion of the traumatic moment. In such moments, when the organism experiences what is dangerous, panic reactions ensue and mobilize defenses.

The difficulty here is, what is danger, what is the traumatic moment? For Freud, this whole situation was explained on the basis of Little Hans — the glasses, the moustache, and the fear of horses. But the danger situations and traumatic moments for girls are ill-defined. In this volume, a range of gender-specific genital anxieties will be delineated that may point to the traumatic moments for the little girl.

These traumatic moments of course are based on the particular anatomical and physiological constellation — the "equipment" — with which the little girl traverses her developmental path. As will be seen, the genital anxieties in the female also have their developmental progression and their specific function in the shaping of psychic structures, and they serve as psychic organizers. Freud emphasizes that the anxiety signal is activated by dangers from both without and, more importantly, within. The genital anxieties having to do with access, diffusivity, and penetration are particular cases in point.

It must be stated that none of these anxieties of experiences of vulnerability are deficiencies. They are affirmations of a positive presence of female identity. Castration implies absence or feeling bereft. There is no denying that such experiences mark the inner lives of men and women alike. It is the nature of female genital anxieties that they also carry with them the sources of activity and, when interpreted, point in the direction of integration and mastery.

THE SHAPE OF THE SUPEREGO
IN WOMEN

One of the major achievements in the development of psychoanalytic theory in the 1920s was the structural point of view, the second typography. One of the more regrettable corollaries was the manner in which the shape of mental structure (notably of the superego) was delineated differentially for the two sexes. In fact, in various well-cited utterances, it was suggested that women are deficient in the development of the superego. All this, of course, was based on the fallacy that differences in kind imply differences in worth.

This distorted view of mental structures is not unique to

psychoanalysis. The idea that qualitatively distinct structures characterize each gender, in spite of evidence to the contrary, was resisted in many spheres of inquiry in the early part of the twentieth century. For instance, anatomy textbooks quite commonly depicted the human homunculus in the brain based on men, not women. And besides anatomy and physiology, sex-linked depictions of human structure are found in characterology as well, in the description of the strong character as male and the weak as female. In the present day, traces of such thinking are found in cognitive science, where such variables as field-independence are linked to males and field-dependence to females. Much of this work has recently been disclaimed, qualified, or corrected, but the division of the strong–weak dichotomy persists and pervades our consciousness and our language — so, too, to a great extent in Freud's writings, including the account of the genesis and functioning of the superego.

Nonetheless, we must not throw out the baby with the bathwater. Freud's concept of the development of mental structure was revolutionary. Indeed, everybody has an id, ego, and superego. Even more important is his conception of the development of the superego as the prototype for the development of mental structure out of an intense object relationship. The ego is not only an evolving nucleus: it grows through identification. As Freud so beautifully put it, the shadow of the object falls upon the ego. His assertion that the superego is the heir to the Oedipus complex implies that confrontation with the parent is an essential precursor to the internalization of structure. Moreover, true psychic structure develops only with genitality. What have been neglected are the gender-specific patterns in the development of that structure.

Within the framework of the classical view of the super-ego, how can one define the gender-specific shape of the female superego and, ultimately, of the male superego as well? To do so, one must eschew the mode of categorical thinking that defines mental structures as strong or weak. The superego, to begin with, is a compromise formation that comprises many psychic constituents, not just genital, but narcissistic, anal, and phallic as well. Thus, instead of the unidimensional description, a superego *profile* can be created, of structure, strength, and content, which reflects its multidimensional shaping. The example of genital anxieties makes it clear that the patterns of vulnerability are distinct for the sexes: no longer can castration be used as the primary model for psychic injury; issues of diffusivity, penetration, and access must be considered on an equal plane.

There is one further issue that needs to be considered in a gender-specific view of the superego, and this has to do with the particular pattern of internalization. To be sure, the very notion of the superego is based on the shadow of the object leaving its mark on the identity of the ego, or self. The formation of psychic structure, however, depends not only on identification, but on disidentification, and here the path for women is quite distinctly different. The processes that are involved in superego formation in the male, which give it some of its impersonal qualities, derive from the extent to which the boy is forced to disidentify from mother: some of the impersonal quality comes from the relinquishing of the object. In contrast, the process of disidentification in the girl is more gradual, occurs later in development, and is not as impersonal. This gradual process of detachment is an important factor in identity formation. In fact, the girl never totally disidentifies from mother, and this implies that the shape of the superego is different. Here the key issue is not castration but the processes of disidentification. This has been neglected in the literature on the female superego. The concept comes from Anna Freud, but even she did not apply it differentially to men and women. We know, of course, of many other gender-specific expressions of the emotions, notably patterns of crying (Greenacre 1953).

There have been several post-Freudian attempts to chart the path of superego development in women. Some are not relevant to a classical conception of the superego. The Kleinian notion of an oedipal struggle during the depressive position deals with superego precursors (cf. Klein 1945). The Lacanian view deals with a language of symbolic notation, which is not readily translatable to current psychoanalytic thought. The most significant contribution to a classical view of the superego is represented in the work of Edith Jacobson (1964). In a pioneering effort, she depicts the unique thrust of the little girl toward superego development. However, she holds onto the notion that the little girl has to accept the inevitability of castration. In fact, Jacobson maintains that because the girl experiences the sense of having been castrated, she is more pliable and obedient as she enters the oedipal phase; she has already suffered the blow and has accepted her fate. Clearly, the traumatic moment is not simply the loss of the imagined phallus. The fundamental issue is that structure formation in women is based on that unique pattern of anxieties specific to their anatomy, and on that unique pathway to identification and disidentification that marks the resolution of the struggle with parental authority.

GENDER MYTHOLOGY, FAIRY TALES, AND THE OEDIPAL SITUATION

Mythology has been a powerful instrument in psychoanalytic thought. We do think by analogies. If an analogy, a scenario, is rooted in 2,000 years of history, and at the same time is applicable to the understanding of a particular life in the here and now, our understanding of that life is indeed persuasive. Conversely, myths are prime examples of how we construct or endow our past, in reconstructive fashion, with those myths or legends, fairy tales or daydreams, that make our existence convincing. This type of thinking has been the cornerstone of Western civilization. It can be found in psychoanalysis in the recurrent use of the Oedipus myth, the Electra myth, fairy tales, and daydreams. Indeed, this line of thinking has led us to reexamine the psychoanalytic understanding of two major myths, those of Oedipus and Electra, as well as an example of fairy tales, the story of Cinderella.

In classical theory, the Oedipus myth is central. In his encyclopedia article, Freud (1923b) declared that he who does not accept the Oedipus complex cannot call himself a psychoanalyst. In some way, we can accept this; in most general terms, there is truth to this, but only if that statement is read in very restrictive terms. It does imply that the inevitable confrontation with the parent (in a triangular sense) is a precondition to structure formation. But the oedipal situation implies far more than that, for it asserts a craving that is specific to each of the sexes. The oedipal myth involves the craving of the boy for his mother and the ensuing guilt. (Note: Doris Bernstein had a strong commitment to work out the female Oedipus complex; Chapter 5 deals with the Electra myth, and the oedipal is not fully worked out there. A fuller treatment can be found in the discussion of Cinderella, Chapter 7.) Should this be the basic template for the understanding of all human development? It is a remarkable phenomenon that the Oedipus myth has become part of the analytic vocabulary, and its companion piece, the Electra myth, has been neglected. If one accepts the notion of gender specificity, then one can find a distinct place for the Electra myth and the female oedipal myth in psychoanalytic thinking.

The delineation of the Electra complex from the female Oedipus complex underscores the psychoanalytic understanding of the female psyche. Manifestly, Electra is enraged at mother for betraying her beloved father, and this appears to imply a triangular relationship. However, Electra's rage at her mother has what would be called today preoedipal overtones — anger at deprivation, at insufficiency and emptiness. More important, the rage is not only at deprivation but is directed at the omnipotent mother. The power that mother has is a source of tremendous outrage. Mother is the queen. Her very queenship, her power, enrages Electra, who mocks the man who lets the woman rule. The fear of the omnipotent mother of course also can be found in males, but to a lesser extent, and its significance is a different one. In some way, this omnipotent mother, or earth mother, is a root of civilization.

There is a further, singular aspect of the Electra myth: namely, that father is absent. The craving for the absent father cannot be equated with the craving for the present father. We would thus have to disagree with those French analysts who assert that an oedipal situation can be found in the earliest phase of development — in the dyad — by virtue of the awareness of the absent father. Such an interpretation would apply to the Electra myth. But the delineation of a female Oedipus complex would have to take a different form.

Psychoanalysis presents two major developmental myths, the oedipal, with the prototype for boys, and the Electra, with the prototype for girls — the latter, unfortunately, eschewed by Freud after it was embraced by Jung. It is unfortunate for a gender-specific view that there is no appropriate triangular myth applicable to women. But as true psychoanalysts, if we don't have it, we construct it. The best we can do at this point is to sketch out how Electra, if she were to be involved in a truly triangular struggle, would differ from her male counterpart, Oedipus. Electra never kills her mother, which is precisely what Oedipus does to his father at the crossroads.

Here again we can span the centuries and move from mythology to the clinical process in the here and now. The distinction between Oedipus and Electra, noted above, is reflected in the different ways males and females cope with aggression. The fear of aggression is an anxiety characteristic of all humans — and yet, it may well be that in the male the wish to attack is dreaded because, in some way, it is governed by the unconscious fantasy, "I really have the power to kill father." The female, on the other hand, if she is governed by Electra's myth, even in her most virulent rage, does not seem to desire the death of her mother. It is as yet an open question whether the destructive and enraged woman is the product of a male fantasy and how much it is the unconscious fantasy of women as well.

DYAD: THE DEEPENING
OF THE CLINICAL PROCESS

So far, the conception of gender specificity has focused on the basic theoretical edifice: notions of development, psychic structure, the nature of anxiety, and the nature of unconscious fantasies. But implicit all along is evidence that these ideas are played out and have a pivotal place in the analytic process itself. The question must be faced: in what way does the actuality of the analyst's gender play a role in the shape of the emerging transference? The message here is, perhaps, analyst beware.

The clinical folklore surrounding the issue of the gender of the analyst has been shrouded by a paradox. On the one hand, there is the view that the unfolding transference scenario evolves, like a deus ex machina, inevitably, and that therefore the gender of the analyst is inconsequential. The alternate view, probably equally erroneous, involves an optimal match, as though gender were all-decisive. "He needs a man" or "she needs a woman" are popular phrases. Such a view, carried to its extreme, would hold that male analysts can never analyze women nor women analysts men. This apparent practical, though not logical, paradox is resolved if we appreciate the role of the partial actuality of the fact of gender in the treatment situation, in the context of, or in interaction with, the patient's unconscious fantasy scenario. Erikson (1962), many years ago, recognized this actuality in the course of Freud's treatment of Dora. His message has not been fully appreciated.

This factor of the partial intrusion of gender actuality works, of course, within the framework of the various combinations in the particular treatment situation: female–female, female–male, male–female, and male–male. Obviously, then, this is not an issue for female analysts alone nor for male analysts, but, in the spirit of gender specificity, an issue that shapes various unfolding patterns within the treatment process. The concept of shape must include the issue of sequence as well: it is quite likely that the actuality of the female analyst in the early phase of treatment favors the development of the maternal transference, and the presence of a male analyst, by extension, of a paternal transference. But, with a deepening of the process, and the analyst's awareness of his or her gender-linked countertransference, the complete preoedipal and oedipal situation becomes part of the clinical process. It is only in this sense that the female analyst can be a good enough analyst for both men and women, and the same holds true for the male analyst.

With this recognition of the actuality of gender and the unfolding of the transference shape over time (Sandler and Rosenblatt 1962), specific gender-linked issues can be noted in the treatment process. In the present volume, this is emphasized for the female–female dyad. Clinical practice makes us readily aware of the broad range of potential pitfalls that emerge in the gender-linked countertransference. There are issues of potential overidentification on the part of the female analyst with her female patient's career goals, or, conversely, failure — especially within the current *zeitgeist* — to empathize with the more traditional gender-linked strivings. The collective countertransference of our female analyst colleagues can be noted in the analytic literature, with the great reluctance to accord women their proper place in the development of the superego. Further, in the area of psychosexual development, the female analyst will find a natural inclination toward receptivity (the very aspect of listening is a process of reception), and yet the act of interpretation can also be an act of penetration.

It is hoped that consciousness of these issues in the treatment process will serve the implicit and explicit function of deepening the analytic process and facilitating the resolution of the transference crisis.

CONCLUSION

All this is designed to provide a frame, a map, of the contours of the gender-specific views. They have been stated so far in theoretical terms. But of course they come to life in the process of living, both in and out of the treatment situation. Thus the entire approach rests on the observation and documentation of the clinical process. It is hoped that gender specificity will come to life in the contents of communicated anxiety, in the patterning of the superego, and in the female and male Oedipus, as this may be seen in dreams, associations, and pivotal moments of treatment, and, most generally, in the process of working through at various points of the treatment process. The concepts are clinical and the data are clinical.

A final word on the plan for this book — the organization is governed less by chronology than by theoretical cogency. The chapter on developmental considerations, Chapter 2, is, in a sense, a precursor chapter, expressed in nontechnical language. It lays the foundation for the gender-specific view within our current social structure and *zeitgeist*. Then follows the genital anxiety chapter, Chapter 3, which is theoretically seminal. While its final publication date is a later one, it was begun earlier and rewritten many times, precisely because of its centrality. The notion of gender-specific anxieties has a bearing on both the male and female superego and the male and female Oedipus complex. How all this is deployed in the clinical situation of the female–female dyad is spelled out in Chapter 6. It is evident that this is only a partial contribution, for surely the consideration of the female–female dyad should be followed by chapters on the female–male and the male–male dyads. But unfortunately, this logical completion of the line of thought enunciated here was not allowed to be.

2

Female Identity
Synthesis

EDITORS' INTRODUCTION

This chapter is a preview of thoughts to come. It was introduced in the context of sweeping cultural changes challenging traditional models of masculinity and femininity, and it was addressed to a broadly based intellectual community. But a careful reading of this relatively early work shows that it contains, in nontechnical language, Bernstein's view of female development, of the superego, of the nature of anxiety, and of the nature of the oedipal situation.

The inspiration for this work came from her listening stance within the framework of the analytic situation. She did not know yet what there was to be worked out, but she knew there was the task of finding a new language for old concepts. The subsequent chapters (Chapter 3 on) represent a systematic endeavor in that direction.

* * * *

We are confronting a cultural upheaval in which the familiar models of masculinity and femininity do not seem viable. In our era many social institutions are in flux; church, state, army, and schools are losing their powerful functions as advisors and protectors. Now traditional models of femininity and masculinity as aids and organizers of developing personalities are crumbling. Educational and career opportunities for women, smaller families, distant families, and divorces are all creating new realities and making new demands on men and women. Ready-made societal solutions to old conflicts are not available, and individuals must find new solutions.

In a sense, the newly emerging demands on the individual are unprecedented; we are asking that each individual find a way to encompass within his or her own ego boundaries and his or her own identity all instinctual derivatives so that each individual will be active, passive, assertive, receptive, and aggressive as the need arises. These changes are evident in clinical work as women are moving into new spheres of activity and are trying to integrate new aspirations with more traditional concepts of themselves as women.

In working with women, I have found them struggling in roles for which there are few precedents. The models of femininity that were presented to them during their childhood do not fit their current adult lives. Most women I have treated were expected to live lives much like those of their mothers (i.e., to be wives and mothers in turn). While many were well educated, they were expected to make use of their education only until they married or in case of financial emergency. In order to meet the challenge of new demands it is necessary that women find a new identity synthesis.

I use the phrase *identity synthesis* instead of *identity* to convey the ongoing process of synthesizing such identity components as gender identity, ego, superego, ideals, and identifications; the concept encompasses a sense of self, a sense of continuity with one's past, and an orientation toward the future.

Every culture provides identity models that are crystallized out of the total range of human feelings, wishes, needs, and aspirations. These models serve society adaptively by meeting cultural needs; they serve the child growing up in the culture as a guide and goal for developing an adaptive character.

Developmental conflicts and early and often unconscious identifications and repressions can facilitate or inhibit later adaptive adult identity experiences. Psychoanalysis, through its study of the child and character formation, can contribute to the understanding of the vicissitudes of childhood out of which a sense of identity emerges (see, for example, Weil 1958).

Freud viewed the emergence of femininity and masculinity as outcomes of the interaction of manifestations of physiological bisexuality and varied identifications as consolidated at the time of the resolution of the oedipal period. Femininity was dependent on the repression of the masculinity in the girl's character and on appropriate identifications with her mother. The boy's masculinity required the reverse — repression of femininity and his identifications with the father. The male repressed his wish to be nurturing and some of his wishes to be nurtured and projected them onto his wife, whose role was to be dependent on him and, at the same time, care for many of his needs. The woman repressed her aggressive, assertive strivings and projected them onto her husband, who was required to be strong, to work, and to provide economically for her. Through these mechanisms of selective repression and mutual projection and the resulting unconscious gratification, masculinity and femininity are defined.

The roles thus defined could be relevant, adaptive, and even mutually gratifying in a culture that was stable and in a marriage that was stable, but they can no longer be adaptive, at least for women, in the changing world of today. The woman who has repressed her assertive, aggressive impulses and has developed her personality along this model often finds herself inadequately equipped to work, to be a divorcee or a widow, or to make her way in the world after child-rearing years (the empty nest syndrome). Confronted with new demands, it is necessary for her to attempt a major reorganization of herself and to create a new identity synthesis.

Autonomy, independence, and assertiveness, the qualities most valued in our society, are considered unfeminine. Women face a dilemma: in order to be feminine, they must relinquish the very character traits and repress the underlying instinctual drives that they later need in order to develop their own potential or even to survive. These traits are admirable in women only when they are exercised in the service of others' needs. In homemaking and child rearing, these qualities are permissible and make the woman who exercises them a "good" woman in her own internal system and in the eyes of the outside world. When she ventures to use them in behalf of her own personal interests or pursuits, however, she loses esteem and femininity. When a woman is called "independent," it is usually in a pejorative tone.

Women are often very anxious in situations that call for aggressive action because aggression is an impulse that has had to be repressed in the developing girl. As their lives are requiring them to behave more assertively, this childhood repression is maladaptive. Women's efforts to cope with this issue are clearly manifest in the assertiveness training groups that have become very popular on a national scale. Men, in response to the changes, are also confronted with considerable anxiety. As they are being asked to take over some of the nurturing toward themselves and their children, they, too, are confronted with a repressed forbidden aspect of themselves. If we consider the resistance by both men and women to the Women's Liberation Movement, it is apparent that anxiety and rage have been generated. The movement undermines the underlying personality structures of both men and women.

I am going to discuss three aspects of female development that I have found contribute to difficulties women are having in the face of the change in values and social patterns in our culture. I will discuss (1) problems in separation-individuation, (2) the nature and contents of the female superego, and (3) problems in forming identifications as they influence the adult identity synthesis.

SOME ISSUES IN SEPARATION-INDIVIDUATION

The first aspect of female identity synthesis is the separation-individuation process. There can be no satisfactory individual identity experience if the child does not develop an awareness of itself as a being physically and emotionally separate from the mother. The establishment and maintenance of psychic individuation, together with core gender identity, forms the basis of the identity experience.

It is often said that women are lacking independence and autonomy, that they are dependent on others, and that they lack individuality and are "followers." Women tend to be defined and to define themselves in terms of their relationships to others. The female is always somebody's object; first she is Mommy's baby doll, then Daddy's darling, later someone's wife, and then someone's mother. This immediately brings into focus a core problem with women; they find it difficult to define themselves without these references.

Those who emphasize social factors will point to cultural pressures on women to remain dependent, even somewhat helpless and childlike, in order to be womanly. Psychoanalysis has stressed the inner conflicts that interfere with individuation. However, I have found it is the fitting or convergence of outer pressures with these inner struggles that makes the individuation process difficult for girls.

I will discuss two major issues affecting individuation in the female: (1) the early relationship with the mother, and (2) the girl's anatomy and its relationship to her psychic experience.

Psychoanalysis records the extraordinary role the mother plays during the child's early infancy in the formation of the self-image. In a kind of mirroring, the infant internalizes the image of itself as it is reflected to the child in the mother's face and in her treatment of the child.

Because of this process, the mother's conscious and unconscious attitudes play a critical role in the girl's experience of herself. Some women do not value a daughter as they would a son. Other women are not valued (by husbands, by culture at large) if they produce daughters and not sons. Still others see *themselves* as devalued and hence can only see their own products (children) as devalued. Whatever the causal factors may be in forming the mother's attitudes, those attitudes powerfully affect the infant girl's sense of self-worth. But, although the mother's attitudes influence much of the content of the child's self-image, I don't think that this factor alone accounts for the girl's difficulty in achieving autonomy so often noted both as a cultural phenomena and as a clinical symptom.

I think there is a factor that transcends the particular

contents of each individual mother's personal values. *All mothers share one common experience: the mother sees herself in the body of her infant daughter.* She relates to her daughter truly narcissistically. The body the mother sees is known and familiar, one with which she can have total identification, one in which she recognizes her own past and present self. In contrast, the boy can only be experienced by the mother as different from herself. There cannot be the deep biological understanding of the male body experience that the mother has with her daughter. We have been accustomed in psychoanalysis to considering the boy as the narcissistic completion of the mother. Although he may be her treasure and prize, his body cannot be something with which she identifies in the same way as she does with the girl's body. (If I were to venture a hypothesis, I would say that part of the mother's relationship to the girl is a reflection of the mother's early narcissism — narcissism on the undifferentiated level. The narcissism she experiences at a later stage in her development appears in relation to her son; it is more object oriented. The son is viewed as her phallic or anal treasure [object] instead of as part of herself.)

It is, I think, self-evident that sameness facilitates sameness and difference facilitates difference. The mother's experience is reflected in the child, who in turn experiences itself as "the same as" or "different from" the mother. The boy experienced as "different from" mother is aided in his path toward individuation in a way not available to the girl. The very structures of the relationships differ.

The contents of the parental expectation resulting from gender assignment further support individuation in the boy and oppose it in the girl. From the moment of gender assignment at birth, the mother expects that the boy will leave her, leave home, and have a career. In the toys given children and in the games played with them, these conscious and unconscious expectations are communicated. The subtle disapproval toward the boy in his nurturance play pushes him from this exercise of the early, automatic identifications with the mother; the encouragement of these activities reinforces this primary identification in the girl.

It has been suggested that the girl has an easier time in establishing and maintaining gender identity (Stoller 1968), but gender identity, although central, is only one aspect of an identity synthesis. The very factor of her likeness to mother that makes it easier for her to maintain gender identity may stand in the way of other, equally important aspects of identity formation.

The second major factor, I think, that plays a role in interfering with the girl's individuation lies in her own body. We are accustomed to saying that the ego is at core a body ego, that is, that the ego develops out of a mental representation of the child's discovery and experience of his or her own body. However, we have generally omitted noting that the body ego includes sexual components. I believe this omission to be the heritage of earlier psychoanalytic theory that hypothesized identical prephallic phases for children of both sexes and omitted the role that sexual differences play in early ego formation and early identity formation. Freud ascribed the observed differences in male and female character to the psychological consequences of the girl's perception that she "lacks" a penis (and all that is implied in terms of castration anxiety or lack of castration anxiety). In early theory, the girl is a "boy" first and becomes a girl following the phallic phase. My thesis is that these observed differences reflect different physiological and psychological experiences during an earlier phase, during separation-individuation.

An early genital phase occurring during the separation-individuation phase has been observed. Once the early genital phase is experienced, it becomes part of the developing child's apparatus for discharge and becomes activated whenever there are stimuli requiring discharge (Roiphe 1968). If we consider the differences in the nature of the female and male sexual experience, they seem to suggest some of the observed differences in male and female functioning. For example, women's cognition has been described as being more intuitive, moving from a sense or feeling toward the cognitive statement, while men's cognition is described as the reverse — the clear, logical thought followed by inner reverberations.

More specifically, I believe these differences have ramifications for problems of individuation. The female sexual experience is a more internal, diffuse, generalized sensation than in the male. Being internal and unseen, it cannot be given a specific physical boundary. In contrast, the male genital experience is specific, local, and focused; the penis can be seen and felt, both tactilely and sensorily. One can act with it and on it. I propose that this kind of different bodily experience serves the individuating boy in a way not available to the girl in the midst of the same psychic development. I am suggesting that the diffuse, internalized, nonspecific nature of the girl's early *sexual* experience is similar to the nonspecific, generalized, undifferentiated *psychic* experience during her early infancy. The boy's sexual experience, with its boundaried specificity, opposes the undifferentiated symbiotic experience and aids in building psychic boundaries from the inside (i.e., within the body experience). In addition, the penis is eminently suited for individuation, because it serves as a natural anatomic vehicle for the drive outward, whereas the girl's excitement leads her inward and back to an earlier psychic state of boundarilessness.

I think this role of the penis is reflected in clinical material. If we listen to women in relation to men, we hear, "Men can travel," "Men can go out in the world," "Men can be independent." What they are really saying is, "Men can go, they can leave." To put these statements into psychoanalytic language relevant to identity formation, what they are saying is that men can separate (individuate) and become separate human beings.

Here, then, is where I would place the famous (or infamous) "Anatomy is destiny" (Freud 1924). *The mother's perception of the girl's anatomy and the power of gender assignment together with the girl's own early diffuse genital experience oppose individuation.* The blurred boundary between self and mother in early infancy is reflected and reinforced by her anatomy. There is a convergence of the girl child's experience in the outer world (first with her mother, then with cultural pressures) and in the inner world (within her own body).

Psychoanalysis has been attacked for the phallocentricity of its theory. It is, however, only a reflection of wide cultural values shared in almost every known culture. Many reasons have been offered to explain the veneration of the male. The issue of psychic individuation, separation from the omnipotent seeming mother of early infancy, seems to provide a universal sphere of reference. *The function of the penis as an aid in individuation may well be a psychobiological origin of universal phallocentricity.* Given the identical gender identity with the mother and the contribution of perception and sensory experience in the sexual sphere, together with culturally determined expectations and pressures, the girl has a more difficult time and fewer supports than the male in the individuation process.

ASPECTS OF SUPEREGO DEVELOPMENT THAT INTERFERE WITH AUTONOMY

Aspects of the female superego contribute to the difficulties women have in achieving an identity synthesis that is adaptive to the cultural scene. Difficulties arise from both the nature of the superego's structure and the contents. There has been confusion between the superego as a structure and the contents of that structure. Structure is an organization of prohibitions and admonitions to control and regulate drives as they are expressed in behavior and character. Content is the specific admonitions and prohibitions, the dos and don'ts. The superego's strength is not determined by the nature of its content, but by how powerfully the structure enforces that content. For example, the superego directive (content) to "be pliant" can create a "pliant" person who appears to have a weak superego; but, in fact, it may take a very strong superego structure to enforce the directive.

Many of the observed differences between the male and female superego are accounted for by the different contents. All of us who work with women know that the superego of women is not weaker than that of men; indeed, it is often tyrannical. Its contents contain character directives to be pliant, be flexible, be obedient, be pleasing, be attentive, and to do as others expect you to do. The prohibitions are: do not be aggressive, do not be assertive, autonomous, or independent. These latter qualities, forbidden to women by a superego that declares that these traits are unfeminine when exercised in pursuit of personal interests, are permitted when they are exercised in the service of others' needs (children, husband, home). Women are expected to be "in attendance." The cultural role may well be a reflection of anatomy in that the woman's body is nurturing, supporting, and feeding. There may be a fitting between the anatomic experience and the cultural expectation. However adaptive this attending model may be for a woman in her nurturing role, it is maladaptive for many of her new aspirations and needs.

Clinically, we repeatedly note that the slightest eruption of aggression or self-assertion causes some women great anxiety. Women in analysis, when confronted by an emerging drive derivative, be it sexual or aggressive, will anxiously ask, "What am I supposed to do?" far more frequently than men, who seem better able to enjoy aggressive and sexual fantasies. Women rarely can elaborate fantasies connected to these drives: "I want to . . . ," "I feel like doing . . . ," "I see myself as. . . ." The assertive *I* brings forth the anxiety because of the powerful superego commandment against such self-assertion. The impulse (aggression, sexuality) would be acceptable if someone (e.g., the analyst) would give permission for its expression. The superego command to follow explains Freud's observation that women often change their standards to conform with those of their lovers. I believe it also largely explains the success of assertiveness training groups, as it is inherent in the title that to be assertive is acceptable and desirable. In psychoanalytic terms, these groups have taken over a superego function (Freud 1921) and are providing new content, "Thou shalt be assertive," in place of the old prohibition. The ideals of the new external group (assertiveness training group) replace the ideals of the old internal group (parents, early cultural influences).

In considering the contents of the female superego one hears a repetition of the conflicts reviewed in the discussion of the separation-individuation process. Whereas the task of separation-individuation is the achievement of autonomy and independence, the contents of the superego for the girl contain directives against full achievement of autonomy. Once again, at this later stage of development, the girl may be pushed back toward the early infantile dependency.

At each stage of development, earlier structures and identifications related to the new ones are revived and influence the new stage of development (Reich 1954). This means that when a little girl's superego is being formed, her early relationship with her idealized mother plays a role. The mother of early childhood is identified with maternal, serving, nurturing qualities because she was totally nurturing to the infant girl and at the beck and call of the infant's needs. This image of the totally nurturing mother (in the experience of the infant who sees the mother only insofar as she serves its needs) is reawakened in terms of what the budding woman *should* be. This infantile image of the all-giving mother, a Mother Earth, is the basis of the ideal mother. Always a distortion resulting from the infant's immature perception, it nevertheless becomes the model for Mother and puts totally unrealistic pressures on women (from inside themselves as well as outside) to conform to this image. This idealized mother of infancy provides the contents of the superego commandments. This explains, I believe, the guilt so frequently encountered in working women when they are not in attendance on their family's needs. I have found intense guilt in women, whether or not they are really neglecting their families; indeed, women tend to feel guilty about the *wish* to work. This resurrected idealized image of what a mother "ought" to be makes a decision very difficult when a woman is faced with a conflict between pursuing her own career interests and the needs or wishes of her family. This idealized image of the good mother is reflected back to the woman in terms of cultural expectation. From the time she is a toddler, the cultural and parental ideal for the girl is that she be soft, pliant, and in attendance on others (i.e., her husband, her children, her parents).

Not only does the revived image of the idealized mother of infancy play a role in the content of the superego commandment for the girl, but the revived relationship also affects the structure. The resurrection of this early relationship also brings a revival of the child's earlier mental state. That early mental state is characterized by confusion; the mother seems all-powerful. These factors affect the formation of the superego. As she was once totally helpless in relation to the omnipotent mother (in her perception), she feels helpless in relation to the superego. As she was once confused in her understanding of the mother's expectations, she feels confused in relation to the superego's commandments.

The idealized mother of early infancy is resurrected for the boy as well as for the girl. His superego commands him to be all-providing, all-protective, and all-powerful. Men are subject to much anxiety and despair when they do not live up to these internal (and external) expectations. Men perceive these male, paternal qualities as being like the powerful fathers of their childhood. But behind the powerful image of the father, one can recognize the mother of the nursery: providing, protecting, and seemingly all-powerful. That image of the mother is distant from the boy's ideal; it is remote, alien, and powerfully defended against. The intervening experiences for the male have transformed this early figure from the mother to the father.

As discussed in the section on separation-individuation, there has been a constant pressure on the boy to disidentify himself from the mother since early infancy. He is encouraged to protect and shelter in ways that are removed from the direct bodily nurturance. The direct expression of these wishes can lead the little boy into the most mortifying ridicule. The impulse to be nurturing may be the same as in the girl, but the form of expression must be quite different. His superego contents are, "Do not be like mother; be like father." Men do not face conflict over working as women do; they are confronted with guilt if they do not work. They seem to have little conflict about time and energy invested in careers, even when little time is left for their families; their work is not in conflict with the ideal images of themselves as fathers.

Freud (1925) described the superego in women: "Their

superego is never so inexorable, so impersonal, so independent of its emotional origins as we require it to be in men" (p. 257). These differences have been ascribed to the absence of castration anxiety in the girl. I think, however, that one might reformulate the source of the differences in terms of the resurrected omnipotent ideal mother of infancy and its effects on both content and structure of the superego. The girl is not so independent of her emotional origins; she is much closer to the early dependency and accompanying mental state. Because of differences throughout the boy's development (particularly separation-individuation), including the transformation of the idealized, grandiose image from the mother to the father, the boy is less susceptible to these early influences. The resulting superego in the boy *is* more distant and impersonal. Although the girl's superego is different, it is not weak. It is quite powerful, in the image of the grandiose mother of infancy. Because of the revived early state, it has the capacity to be less rigid; it is not weak, but rather it is flexible.

To reiterate, at the stage of superego development, both the boy and girl are subject to the resurrected idealized image of the mother and the early mental states that characterized that period. Because of the differences in development, the boy is not as susceptible to these influences encompassing nurturing aspects and the ego diffusion that accompany the early stages. The boy is more resistive to regressive influences, while the girl has no place to go but back. The revival of the earlier states gives the female superego a different characteristic than that of the male; it has the capacity for greater flexibility. The female superego is not weak, either structurally or in terms of contents. However, because of its different structure and contents, it does oppose the aims of autonomy and assertiveness that women are trying to attain.

PROBLEMS IN FORMING ADAPTIVE
IDENTIFICATIONS

Analytic literature has, for several decades, been preoccupied with the role of the mother in the child's development. The father, central to most of the theories of Freud and his contemporaries, appears to have faded from his once critical role. Analyses of women have mostly been directed at analyzing the conflicts, rivalries, and rages that have interfered with the girl's "proper" identification with her mother. Analyses of women's relations to their fathers have been aimed at resolving those envies and conflicts toward men that have kept them from having "feminine" lives.

But inasmuch as today's young woman needs to go beyond this aim, the traditional suppression of "masculinity" in the girl's character is maladaptive, and the father must be considered not only as an erotic object, but as an object of identification and ego resource. Psychoanalysis has not addressed itself sufficiently to this aspect of the role of the father. (For an interesting discussion, see Leonard 1966.)

As the girl identifies with her father and he emerges as an ego resource, considerable anxiety is aroused in both parents. There are in operation massive cultural prohibitions against individuals behaving in ways that differ from the sex role models. I call these prohibitions *forbidden identifications*. The girl who wishes to identify with aspects of her father must deal with anxiety and conflict in relation to both parents and society, and within herself.

Considerable conflict may arise between mother and daughter if the daughter wishes to break with familiar female roles and develop a career. The threat to the mother is twofold. First, she must "lose" her daughter; when the girl goes off into the career world, she leaves home, physically and emotionally. When girls remained at home, they were safe from the conflicts over separation; so were their mothers. Neither mother nor daughter had to face the pain and loss of leaving.

"You have a son 'till he gets a wife; You have a daughter all your life." When the daughter chooses a career, she is interrupting the generational repetition of women in the home; the mother–daughter tie perpetuated by the daughter's continuing the mother's role is broken.

Second, the mother's entire character structure as described earlier is threatened. Her repressions of autonomy, aggression, and aspirations for success in the outer world are threatened by the daughter who refuses to relinquish these aspects of herself. The stimulation of these long-quieted feelings in the mother causes her considerable agitation and anxiety as the defensive structure is threatened.

Patients have described their mothers' reactions to their career aspirations: "Mother ignored me as if I hadn't spoken"; "She seemed to feel betrayed"; "They always worried about what my brothers would do when they grew up, never about us girls"; "I don't think my mother ever 'saw' me"; or "I never came into focus." Such statements often include boundary references either implicitly or explicitly. Issues of being seen, heard, and focused all imply an identity reference. Women who have surrendered their own autonomy and independence in obedience to personal and cultural ideals cannot tolerate the expression of these affects in their daughters. For daughters who wish to have for themselves some of the "masculine" qualities, the traditional balance (through projection and unconscious identification) is upset. Women who have surrendered their autonomy in order to "be women" are threatened by the Equal Rights Amendment (ERA) as much as men are. Their ego boundaries have had to exclude autonomy in order to achieve inner grace with their mothers and their fathers; they cannot welcome it in their daughters.

In forming critical identifications a mother–daughter conflict arises from within the daughter herself. When the girl is in the oedipal phase and later when she is in adolescence, she has the task of forming *appropriate* identifications with her mother. Residues of the symbiotic phase are revived, as mentioned in the discussion of superego formation, and they complicate these identifications. When we hear of perpetual storms between mother and daughter during these stages, I think we are seeing a constant exercise of the *no* muscle. Spitz (1957) described the toddler's *no* as containing an individuating statement, "No, I am not you, or like you"; here the child is aspiring toward autonomy. The girl, during the oedipal and adolescent stages, is struggling simultaneously to attain or retain individuation (be different) at the same time that she is forming identifications with her mother to consolidate her femininity. She is caught in tremendous conflict, trying simultaneously to be *unlike* (retain autonomy) and to be *like* her mother (retain femininity).

This conflict accounts for many of the endless mother-daughter battles in childhood and adolescence. The familiar interpretation of these battles as being the result of competition for the father is yet another expression of analytic phallocentricity.

If the girl were able to use the father as an ego resource and identify with his ability to leave mother, the intensity of much of the girl's struggle would be relieved. Many fathers do not seem able to do for their daughters what they do so readily for their sons (i.e., offer an alliance, a friendship, an identification model).

Daughters who turn to their fathers as an ego resource frequently arouse deep anxiety in them. Men's protection of masculine territory from women is a well-known cultural phenomena reflected in men's schools, clubs, and bars. This need to keep women out is a reflection of the male's need to protect his boundaries (separation-individuation). When this need to keep women out and away extends to the daughter who has a wish or need to identify with his ability to leave (separate from) the mother or to succeed in the outer world, it leaves the girl child without supports for her aspirations. Recent documentation of the role of mentors (Sheehy 1976) for successful women demonstrates how women have found this identification figure in the world when their fathers have not provided it.

Lax (1977) describes several cases in which fathers permitted their daughters to identify with them professionally while still depreciating femininity as a whole and their mothers in particular. These fathers made their daughters "exceptions" by encouraging them in professional spheres while simultaneously devaluing women as love objects. As a result, these women, whose histories Lax traced, were in constant conflict. They could not identify with their devalued mothers; at the same time, identifications with their fathers could only be made at the cost of their femininity. They were split in their sexual, professional, and maternal lives. They were able to find little gratification, even sequentially, but remained in constant conflict, unable to find peace either as wives, mothers, or at work. In other words, these women were unable to achieve an adaptive identity synthesis.

In discussing separation-individuation problems, I discussed the different sexual experiences in the boy and girl. The boy often relies on the anatomical difference to establish individuation. In essence, he says, "I am not one with the nurturing mother. See, I am different." The more the male defines and defends his individuation and his maleness based on the different sexual anatomy, the less likely he is to open his ego boundaries and welcome identifications by his daughter. It is not the penis itself (castration anxiety), but the penis as proof of individuation, that must be guarded and protected. Or, it is not the penis, but *individuation,* which is being protected by use of the penis.

Cultural and analytic phallocentricity are quite profound.

Phallocentric men and women are unable to see the vagina as
an active organ. They see only the penis as active. Why is
there this almost universal insistence that the female lacks an
"executive organ" (Nagera 1975) and that only the penis is
active?

It has been proposed that insistence on the phallus as
powerful is necessary to both sexes to overcome being
helpless at the hands of the once all-powerful mother
(Chasseguet-Smirgel 1970, Schafer 1974, Torok 1970). Not
only was the mother powerful in the infantile psychic
experience, but in traditional homes with the father absent at
work, the mother wielded great power in the day-to-day
routines of life. The powerlessness of the developing child is
quite total; the father becomes a symbol of strength and
power over the mother. He leaves the mother; he has sexual
power over her. In other words, phallocentricity ensures that
someone is stronger than mother, who was once stronger
than everybody. The penis, then, gives assurance that such
power does exist in the world and that those who possess the
penis have that power. As the mother needs to be overpowered to ensure against psychic helplessness, the vagina as a
symbol of the powerful mother must also be denied its
activity. As the omnipotent psychic mother threatens psychic
reengulfment, the vagina becomes the symbol of physical
reengulfment. Thus both men and women must preserve
men's prerogatives as a vehicle of power to reverse the
powerlessness of early infancy. The girl who wishes to
identify with her father challenges this function, and, hence,
there is a culturally forbidden identification of the girl with
her father.

In addition to coping with forbidden identifications, girls
themselves find it difficult to identify with their fathers. The
most obvious difficulty stems from biological differences; in
the same way that mother responds to the like and unlike

qualities of her infants, so does the developing girl feel unlike her father.

I have found that a welcoming paternal attitude either from the father or a significant male figure, such as a mentor, or perhaps later in the analytic transference situation, has facilitated the critical identifications. Fathers, mentors, and analysts can recognize and welcome the girl's interests and activities and provide an ego resource. *It is important that this movement toward the significant male not be misinterpreted as erotic.*

The synthesizing of critical identifications with both mother and father is a difficult task; it requires the girl to be flexibly in touch with different aspects of herself. To be feminine and yet assertive, to work and yet be able to nurture requires a great deal of libido and strength and flexibility to fulfill both roles adequately.

Psychoanalytically, we must be cognizant of forbidden identifications operating from parents and society toward the girl child. We have from the mother, out of her competitiveness, "Do not be like me" and, out of the protection of her image of femininity, "Don't be like your father" and "Don't leave me." From the father we have the classical depreciating attitude toward women that makes it hard for the girl to be like mother but, simultaneously, we have from the father "Do not be like me" (stay out of my territory). I think attention to these conflicting identifications and the facilitating transferential environment in which the female can successfully identify with both parents and be feminine and yet find the gratification available in the world is something to which analysts must be attuned. In a way we must be the carriers of the facilitating identifications for the woman to achieve a rewarding, fulfilling, and yet feminine identity synthesis.

3

Female Genital Anxieties, Conflicts, and Typical Mastery Modes

In "Inhibitions, Symptoms and Anxiety" (1926), an essay that informs all contemporary psychoanalytic thinking, Freud outlined two ways of viewing anxiety. First, he introduced a new theory, signal anxiety; second, he introduced a developmentally based hierarchical conception of anxiety that has the concept of genital anxiety at its apex. Genitality has become a watershed on the path to psychic maturity; the recognition of the differentiation between maleness and femaleness, the attainment of one's own relative wholeness vis-à-vis the object, and the tolerance for conflict are the rewards of this achievement.

Freud outlined age/phase specific dangers, with separation anxiety from the maternal object or figure as the paradigm for subsequent anxieties; he conceptualized phallic phase anxieties differently for boys and girls. For boys, anxiety lay in the threat to their body integrity specifically in castration anxiety (derived from separation from the penis); for girls the danger lay in loss of love of the object (derived from separation from the object). There was no recognition of the role that the girl's own genitals may play in her development or in generating anxiety. Nor does Freud give any recognition to the differences that would follow from such dramatically different formulations; his formulations define the boys' anxieties as much more narcissistically oriented and define the girls' anxieties as much more object embedded.

One of Freud's most brilliant achievements, and that which differentiates psychoanalysis from other perspectives, is that it unifies psyche and soma. Body and soul, mind and body had in previous psychologies and philosophies been perceived as separated, if not outright antagonistic. Freud achieved a conceptual unity, a comprehensive, complementary interdependence between the body and the psyche; they function as one. Indeed, he elaborated the profound and ongoing impact of the body on the development and functioning of the psyche, on character formation, on critical superego differences (see Chapter 4), and on relationships with others. Having recognized and included the body's role in psychic development, it is ironic that it should be just one, the male, whose experience has become the model for human psychology, and only the boy's anxieties and developmental crises the model for all human developmental crises.

At no time did Freud consider the impact of the girl's own body on her psychic development. He considered her genital awareness to be limited to her preoccupation with the penis and her body image based on its absence. In describing genital anxiety (1926), genital is equated with phallus, and the girl's genital is dismissed. "Where castration has already taken place" (p. 125), anxiety occurs in relation to the object. It is as if she had no genital of her own. Indeed, Freud considered early childhood to be identical for boys and girls until the phallic phase, when the girl's discovery that she lacked the valued penis became the central organizer of her psychic life. He considered her own genitals inert, inactive, unknown, not to be discovered until their maturation in puberty. This position was challenged quite early by analysts. Horney (1924) considered the undiscovered vagina to be a repressed vagina; Mueller (1932), originally a pediatrician, reported girls' early genital interest. Reports of childhood masturbation abound in the literature (see Clower 1976). Kestenberg (1956a) has described the ebb and flow of infant girls' genital excitement; Erikson discussed the girl's "inner space" (1964) as her preoccupation with her inner genital. More recently Stoller (1968) and Money and Ehrhardt (1972) have demonstrated that gender identity is established long before the phallic phase and that there is no evidence to sustain Freud's position that the little girl considers herself *un homme manqué.* Despite these observations about little girls' genital awareness and interest, their genital anxiety has always been described as castration anxiety, a legacy of Freud's earlier formulations.

If we do agree that the body is centrally involved in children's psychic development, it seems appropriate that the girl's body, her experiences with it and conflicts about it, are as central to her development as the boy's body is to his. As the bodies are different, the nature of the resulting anxieties, the developmental conflicts, the means of resolution, and many of the modes of mastery must of necessity be different as well.[1]

---

[1]I am using the phrase *modes of mastery* to describe the engagement and integration of developmental tasks. Like crawling, drinking from the cup, walking, and acquiring language, integrating the body image, including the genitals, into the psyche is a necessary developmental achievement. Defense is the more usual psychoanalytic term, but it always implies danger and conflict. While any developmental task, particularly the integration of the genitals into the self-image, can

These anxieties, conflicts, and modes of mastery have a pervasive impact on the resolutions of all childhood developmental tasks, the achievement of separation-individuation, the development of autonomy, the formation of the superego, and the critical identification and resolution of the oedipal crisis.

The issues surrounding girls' and women's reactions to the penis, that is, penis envy and castration anxiety, are described, documented, and elaborated in the psychoanalytic literature. Full discussions abound. Here I will try to separate out the two issues deriving from the role of anatomy in the girl's development. I will attempt to define and explore the impact of her own genitals, assessing their centrality. I will discuss her reactions to the penis only insofar as these reactions affect her integration of her own body image and experience. While several authors (Barnett 1966, Keiser 1953, 1958, Montgrain 1983, Mueller 1932) have addressed female genital anxieties, I am attempting to understand their role in her psychic development, thus viewing her genitals to be as important to her as the boy's genitals are to him. While Galenson and Roiphe (1976) have recently studied toddlers' reactions to the sight of opposite sex genitals, they have viewed their material from the standpoint of a "genital equals phallic" perspective and have not addressed the issue of integrating the girl's own genitals into her body ego. Their conclusions reaffirm Freud's phallic orientation, although placing the recognition of the differences between the sexes at an earlier age. The timetable is significant since the children studied were between 18 and 24 months old, the

---

become conflictual, thereby motivating defense, I do believe there are aspects of each task that are conflict free (Hartmann 1939), simply requiring integration into the ongoing developmental process. "Mastery" seems to me a more appropriate word to describe aspects of developmental integration than "defense."

same age that Stoller (1968) places for the establishment of core gender identity. Thus, this discovery of genital differences takes place in the traditional anal phase or in the phase of separation-individuation. It is my thesis that the task of integrating one's own genital into one's body image interacts with these other developmental tasks and that some of the anxieties the girl experiences at this time are the result of her struggles with her own body experience. Generally speaking, the female has been described as an open system and the male as a closed system (Kestenberg 1956a). In this chapter I attempt to explore some of the implications of this formulation.

ACCESS, PENETRATION, AND DIFFUSIVITY ANXIETIES

The genital anxieties of girls are not nearly as focused and tidy as boys' anxieties. The boy's penis, with its clearly defined presence, contours, visibility, sensations, and vulnerability, is quite clear. The girl's genitals differ in every respect. It is my impression, also noted by other observers (Keiser 1953, 1958, Montgrain 1983), that these differences have multiple effects on psychic structuring and forming mental representations that have pervasive influences on female mental functioning.

I do not mean to suggest that castration-like anxieties do not appear in women; these refer to a host of fears and fantasies about lost, damaged, or missing parts of the body. I have found these ubiquitous in the analyses of women. However, I have not found that they serve exclusively or even dominantly to describe women's genital anxieties. I am proposing three terms, each of which contains several components and references, a far more complex constellation than "castration." *Access, penetration,* and *diffusivity* seem to describe several clusters of female genital anxieties.

Access refers to several different experiences. The girl herself does not have ready access to her genitals, which touches on many levels of experience. She cannot see them as she and the boy can see the boy's genitals. This creates immense difficulty in forming a mental representation of parts of her body in which there are most intense physical sensations. The role of sight in forming mental representations is critical; for example, it has been found that blind children show marked developmental delay in forming body ego/self-images (Fraiberg 1968, Kestenberg 1968).

In addition to the visual difficulty, she does not have complete tactile access to her own genitals; she cannot touch and manipulate them in a desexualized way as can the boy. Hence, she does not acquire tactile, familiar, and sensual knowledge of her body that is not forbidden or tied to forbidden fantasies. Moreover, when she does touch her genitals, there is a spread of sensation to other areas; wherever she touches, yet another area is stimulated. Location shifts not only within the genital, from clitoris to vagina, but to pelvis and to urethral and anal sensations as well. This stimulation spread for the girl contrasts with that of the boy, in whom stimulation focuses.

This spread of sensation leads to a second anxiety, that of *diffusivity*. Development requires the child to define and articulate its body and its world. Touching, seeing, controlling, manipulating and naming (Kleeman 1976) are the equipment with which children build up mental representations of their own bodies, the outer world, and their power and control over themselves, people, and things. If, indeed, ego is at core a body ego, and body ego is an essential reference to the outer world, the diffuse nature of the girl's genital has a significant impact on the nature of her development. Montgrain (1983) discussed this diffusivity in adult women; he noted a "general understatement of the overflowing capacity of women's sensuality that escapes the bind of language." Further, "the insufficient anchorage is an anatomical reality and has a correlative effect on the symbolic level" (p. 170). Language and imagery are essential for women to build a symbolic world that can be controlled and managed. Under stimulation, the entire apparatus of mind and body is mobilized so that a mind–body interaction that underlies thinking can be reactivated under any stress (see also Keiser 1958). It is extraordinary how frequently one hears, in women's analyses, complaints that when they are under stress, particularly intellectual, they cannot "think straight," their minds blur, they get "fuzzy," or they experience an incapacity to articulate. One hears equally often that, after an initial "blank," they are surprised to find how much they really "know" about a given topic, and how much knowledge they had "tucked away." The ordinary senses, sight and touch, are insufficient for girls at this stage of their development. They must rely on additional means, which I will describe fully later as modes of mastery, to articulate and integrate their genitals into their body image.

The third and central cluster of anxieties centers around issues of *penetration*. The vagina is a body opening over which there is no control over opening or closing as there is with the mouth and anus; girls feel they cannot control access by others or by themselves. The fantasy of the genital as "hole" is based on the child's experiences with holes in the external world. They are, indeed, passive and inert. Little girls cannot imagine their genitals' functions and cooperation in coital and childbirth experiences; the lubrication and elasticity of their organs are unknown. This contrasts with the boy's awareness of changes in his organ as part of his daily experiences. The penis and testes respond visibly to temperature and to tactile and erotic stimulation. Girls experience genital excitement as heat, or an itch, or a discomfort, often without awareness of the genesis and often without visible or tactile cause. It is frightening to have an open hole into which things can come and go, and which there is no way to close or open, and no control over access. A derivative appears in a woman, who, angry at her lover, demands the return of her key, so that "he has no access to me." Other openings, the mouth and anus, may be drawn into efforts to master the genital.

One implication of the girl's lack of control over access to her genital is awareness that the access can put her into penetration danger. Not only can things go in and come out, but she fears harm from these things. Girls fear damage to their little bodies from the exciting paternal penis. And, very early, they fear damage to their bodies from the babies they long to create.

Girls struggle with definition and boundaries. Boundaries provide definition and mediate access. The imagined penetration carries not only fear of harm but also arouses anxiety about the crossing of the body boundary. Intercourse requires entry to the inside of the body that can threaten newly established or confirmed body integrity.

Two additional anxieties arise during adolescence when the girl is confronted with wetness for which she knows no source (indeed many adult women do not) and menstruation. Wetness necessarily invokes a regressive potential to all the anxieties and conflicts surrounding early bladder and sphincter control, a full discussion of which is beyond the scope of this work.

It is important to consider the changed timetable for the discovery of anatomical differences and the establishment of gender identity in order fully to appreciate the impact that these anxieties about access, penetration, and diffusivity have on girls' development and the role that they play in women's psyches.

Stoller has demonstrated rather convincingly that gender identity is established by 15 to 18 months of age. Galenson and Roiphe (1976) have noted the recognition and reaction to genital differences at approximately the same time. Hence the discovery and integration of genital differences falls into an already established, though perhaps rudimentary sense of gender identity. These developments take place during the period of development classically considered the anal phase, from Mahler's standpoint (Mahler et al. 1975), the phase dominated by strivings toward separation-individuation. In the realm of cognition, the rapid development of language gives articulated, symbolic form to the developing sense of self and world. In the families of many women with whom I have worked, there is no specific name given to the female genitals (see Lerner 1976, Silverman 1981). Phrases like "down there," "boopee," and "hokee" describe the entire genito-urinary anatomy. One woman assures me that in her language (a sophisticated Indian dialect), no word for the female genital exists, whereas there is a word for the penis.

The integration of genital differences has an impact on all the developmental tasks and particularly complicates the process of separation-individuation for girls. All the genital anxieties I have just described bring unique problems to phase-specific struggles. The separation-individuation struggle is played out in two directions — in relation to the girl's own body and in relationship to her mother. This interplay affects the girl's efforts at mastery. It is my impression that the achievement and maintenance of separation-individuation is the central developmental issue for girls.

FEMALE MASTERY EFFORTS

This variety of specific female anxieties focusing on issues of access, control, and definition is central to the developmental task of achieving individuation. There seem to be specific developmental efforts at mastery that are typical in female development. These are different from the mastery efforts in boys and not aberrations of them. Galenson and Roiphe (1976) have noted differences in boys' and girls' reactions to their observations of genital differences. "The boys reflected the effect of the genital emergence in their choice of those toys and play activities which are usually considered typically masculine, and in the onset of a mild degree of hyperactivity. Furthermore, their masturbation was continued and fairly vigorous from then on." They describe this as "low incidence of overt reaction." By contrast, "all 35 girls in our research sample showed a definite and important reaction to the discovery . . . and eight . . . developed extensive castration reactions" (pp. 46–47). First, I think it is incorrect to describe these boys as having a low incidence of overt reaction; it is more correctly characterized as a more uniform and specific reaction. Their concern is clearly with the penis; their reaction is active, stimulating, in control, self-reassuring and perhaps even counterphobic. This *is* their attempt at mastery over anxieties aroused by genital differences. The activity observed was paralleled by an increase in identification with their fathers. Rather than characterize the girls as having important reactions while the boys had none, it would seem more accurate to describe these reactions as quite different.

The girl is confronted with a different task—she must comprehend, integrate, and locate what is beyond sight, touch, focus, and control. I am suggesting that she mobilizes specific mechanisms to perform this task.

The internal, spreading quality of her sensation quickly and automatically arouses anal and urethral confusion. Galenson and Roiphe report observing oral-regressive behavior, anal zone exploration, and masturbation. I view these turns to these zones not only as regressive but also as a potential turn to modes of mastery. Manipulation, opening and closing and control of access, and holding in are all possible in these body areas.

The following material illustrates the ways in which our usual ways of organizing material can distract us from other essential aspects. The "phallic equals genital" formulation informs both Parens and colleagues (1976) and Galenson's and Roiphe's (1976) work, masking the girl's own genital anxiety about being open and her need to feel in control. Parens described this in his report of 2½-year-old Candy, who, after exposure to sex differences, became markedly preoccupied with a hole in her sock, and, troubled and distressed, tried to make the hole go away. When her mother sewed up the hole, Parens described her as seeming relieved and able to leave her preoccupation and join other children in play.

Following this incident, Candy, although previously toilet trained, began having accidents in which she wetted and then suffered much distress and shame. She then reached for and clung to a large doll, and then showed concern about broken things and wanted only whole crackers. She then "sought the help of her mother and staff to effect a return of her toileting controls" (pp. 88–89). This description was considered by Parens to be ample evidence that Candy was in the phallic phase. What this seems to describe more accurately is that Candy was preoccupied with a hole that she could not close, that this led to regressive wetting that she could not control, and anxiety about things being intact. There is not reported in this material a particular fear of loss of something or damage to her body that would warrant the interpretation of phallic anxiety, nor does there seem to be any justification for describing this as her genito-urinary concerns, that is, her *castration complex. They are not the same.* After her turn to her mother for help in regaining control, "ample genital masturbation emerged" (pp. 88–89). Anxiety aroused an array of reactions in Candy; mastery had to precede the pleasure—here a much more complicated route than for the boy, involving *confusion, regression, loss of control, panic,* and *a turn to others* before a resynthesis, including the genitals, permitted the emergence of genital pleasure that was so readily, directly available to boys. Parens's description seems to support the complexity of the girl's task; "castration" does not do justice to the richness of the girl's experience.

Similar issues are illustrated in the dream of an adult woman during analysis.

This woman has particular difficulty in articulating her genital experiences. Raised in a very strict Catholic boarding school, she was trained to dress and undress without looking at or touching her own or other girls' bodies. Such prepubescent and adolescent activities as self and mutual exploration and mirror looking were all suppressed as were the infantile sexual explorations in her repressive home.

She dreamed that there was a snake in her apartment; she was scared and didn't know where it was, fearing that it would touch her. There was a woman psychologist in a wheelchair but the patient was not sure she could help since she had some kind of illness or disability. I interpreted the dream as follows. She was frightened of having her husband touch her sexually and she was worried whether I, a woman whom she saw as a weak, disabled creature, would be able to help her with her fear, which focused on the fact that she didn't know where "it" was. The patient, who had been quite depressed and listless, came to the next session with the first smile seen in two years of work, and with a twinkle told me of a sudden renewed interest in the stock market, of some trades she had made in the intervening day, of her contemplating buying a seat on a new exchange, which she would *control,* but not necessarily use herself, and earn money by renting the seat to others who wanted to trade. Her movement was clearly to a position in which she did not feel helpless, but could control, manipulate, and enjoy; clearly she resurrected an anal position. To have focused on her perception of me as castrated and disabled would have put the two of us together in a helpless heap. She was afraid, not only of her husband's penis, but of sex in her own body. Would I be able to help her with the scary sex that she couldn't see and that could dart out from anywhere?

Like Candy, frightened by the invisible sexuality, my patient regressed to a mode in which she had already established control (her old interest in the stock market) and turned to an object (the analyst) to help her in establishing not only control but pleasure. For Candy, for my patient, for all little girls, this threatening temporary disorganization must be tolerated by the mother, and the subsequent forward movement toward erotic investment must be welcomed both by mother and father.

Debby, a 24-year-old woman in psychoanalytic therapy, demonstrates a confluence of several of these issues.

Unable to have sexual intercourse for five years, following a half-dozen experiences in college that were relatively successful but accompanied by some bleeding, Debby broke dates, stayed at home, and had eating binges. She described her genitals as a "mystery" and felt that they were damaged, concretized in the memory of a bicycle accident before menarche at the age of 12. She had fallen off her bike into a split with vaginal bleeding. The accident and subsequent medical examination were painful, but there was no medical damage. Nevertheless the memory came up repeatedly as proof of a damaged state. She became sexually aroused on dates, but then tightened her genitals and felt "no one can enter me, I am too tight." Attempts at intercourse were indeed unsuccessful. Her mother had warned Debby against sexual activity until marriage so that she could have control over the man. Her mother also told her not to buy the fur coat she wanted, to wait and let a man buy her one. The therapist began to focus her interventions on Debby's being in control of her pleasures rather than things being done to her or for her. A visit to a gynecologist for a diaphragm brought associations to worries that her hole is not big enough to have anything go in and a disbelief that her vagina could stretch to accommodate either penis or baby. She watched in the mirror as she practiced with her diaphragm, but still was anxious about not seeing her "insides." The therapist empathized with her longing to see but encouraged her to define her sensations by feel and touch. Throughout this period (about 3 months) there was a weight loss of about 8 pounds and a sense of stabilization about food, although neither had come up for manifest work.[2] The therapist interpreted her weight loss in terms of her efforts to control her other opening, her vagina. The therapist worked simultaneously on issues of separation from her mother; Debby recognized her own difficulties in feeling separate from her mother when there was disagreement between them. The confluence occurred when she had successful, pleasurable intercourse, she in a new position, on top (more in control). She longed to run and tell her mother but did not act. The focus on her control of her own body, her genitals, led her to integrate both sex and food with a sense of mastery and separateness from her mother.

The material I have just described focuses on the efficacy of regression and identification in achieving mastery over the elusive genital and the contribution this can make in developing a sense of mastery. There are other mechanisms girls use for dealing with the internal confusion, some potentially considerably less adaptive. While all the mechanisms I am describing here are also found in boys, it is because they carry an extra burden for the girl in her development that I am emphasizing them in this context.

Renunciation of sexuality (Jacobson 1964) is another mechanism utilized by girls when confronted with sexuality

---

[2]A colleague with whom I have discussed this material has found it useful clinically to interpret the oral disturbance in terms of vaginal control issues.

and unsatisfactory pregenital development to support the new demand. The girl who renounces sexuality often turns into a character type we often meet, who is her boss's right arm, her father's nurse, a woman who has an intense but desexualized relationship to usually an older man (Chasseguet-Smirgel 1970).

Another of the mechanisms for mastery of this internal body confusion is externalization, elaborated by Kestenberg (1956a). Onto the doll, which is already a beloved baby and self, is projected erotic investment. Kestenberg finds that play changes to genital-urethral preoccupation; there is more bathing, wiping, and examining in contrast to earlier feeding and cuddling. Girls externalize onto other objects. They develop preoccupation with manipulating and collecting crayons and pens, sometimes the father's. While this preoccupation is considered to be a manifestation of a penis envy response to genital differences (Galenson and Roiphe 1976, Kestenberg 1956a, 1968), I would emphasize a different interpretation of the search for manipulable objects. I see this behavior as an extension of the need for concretization, control, and mastery of the undefined as demonstrated by the fantasy frequently found clinically: "I have a penis, one will grow, it is hidden inside."

Penis envy and fantasy penises can be conceptualized as extremely adaptive fantasies in the girl *at this time* (italics added). Confronted with intense sensations in the genital area, to see the boy's penis and think, "Ah, that's what causes these sensations" is a sensible and imaginative fantasy that can bring order to chaos. As with other childhood fantasies, it should be reworked and absorbed in the process of normal development. The presence and use of the fantasy varies. For example, an adult female patient had a dream: "I am riding in a car with a man and am growing more and more sexually aroused. I look down at my crotch and see an erect penis. I think to myself, 'How else will he know that I am sexy?' " A pregnant woman, who had just associated to penises said, "It's just so nice to think something solid that you can imagine is in there. It's always so vague to think about my vagina." The penis may become an object of covetousness because its fantasied possession is a coherent, cognitive, adaptive explanation for multiple sensations. In fact, there are times when it seems that "having a penis" means having sexuality itself — as a concrete, visible, boundaried word concept. Having a concrete image and a word, that is, language, is an essential part of the ego development that children undergo at this time, and the acquisition of language is inherent and intrinsically linked to the child's ability to manipulate images and ideas. The fantasies that should be transient during the early genital and phallic phases can become central and the girl may be unable to absorb them. What should be transient becomes fixed, leading to either manifest or covert phallic feminine organization and to a girl who lacks access to her femininity.

Ms. A., an accomplished professional woman, always felt a fraud. Analysis revealed the common unconscious equation of "brains equals penis." Intense envy colored relationships with male colleagues who seemed to her to be able to think and work easily and without conflict, and with great conviction of the value of all their utterances. During a session she described all that she admired and envied in a male colleague — his height, his agility, his strength, his clear thinking, his clear lectures. She complained bitterly how much she envied all these attributes. I pointed out one significant omission that really differentiated them, namely his penis, the lack of which in her experience gave her thoughts and lectures a feeling of inauthenticity. She responded by saying she could never relinquish her "phallic" brain and her competitiveness; without them, what would motivate her in her work? After a few minutes silence, she reported an image of a baby sitting in a corner of a playpen: I asked her what the baby was doing. Her response was that the baby was biting the wooden bars; her mother often told her she had done that. I responded by saying that I thought she was answering her own question; she didn't need a fantasy penis, she could "sink her teeth" into a problem, she was not lacking instruments for mastery.

An illustration of a woman's concerns appears in the dreams of a 40-year-old woman in analysis who had been commenting upon her recent and unusual lack of interest in sex, and complaining about her lover's frequent interest.

I have a wound on my hand. I have been bitten — several bites — but it's not bleeding. It becomes like a slash — I can see inside the tissue, the tendon — there is a skin graft done — two pieces in front, one in back of it — one from me — one brown skin — it all fits beautifully — very clean and tidy — but the two men helping are not being careful to be antiseptic. If they are not careful, there will be infection. The next scene is funny. There is this machine examining the inside of a toilet bowl — I think "hey, this thing is an X-ray machine." I can hold up my hand [she holds up the same one she used to illustrate the bite/slash] and you can see the inside — then I put my head in front of it and you can see the inside, but what is clear are the lips, which seem very bright red.

This is a complex dream; I present it because of the many elements of anxiety expressed. The bite, the dirt, the slash, the men who are not careful, the machine that "sees" but can be dangerous. As we can gather from "it's not bleeding," the patient comments that she is menstruating at this time. In addition, in both dream scenes, *one can see inside*. This element repeats in relation to the hand wound, the inside of the toilet bowl, and again with the X-ray, the hand and the head. An analysis of all elements is of course necessary. It would be an error to focus only upon the obvious. The patient herself commented, "I know that the slash is equated with the vagina — that's so classic," with little concern, affect, or conviction. My noting how frequently in the dream she was *looking* and could see inside brought forth more intense feelings. It is of note that this woman, a physician, had recently been expressing worry about not identifying organs correctly during surgery, an anxiety for which there had been no reality base as her familiarity with anatomy was in no way deficient. The patient had begun a menstrual period the prior day, was casual about birth control, and was somewhat concerned about her fertility. Her dream responds, "There is no blood, the bites are easily repaired, how clean, how tidy! All is well." The dream illustrates the confluence of material drawn into genital anxiety and the varied mechanisms attempted to master it; prominent is her wish to see, which must be given equal attention with the more familiar interpretation that she feels her genitals are wounded. This not incorrect but incomplete interpretation leaves the female in the helpless condition so often attacked by critics of castration anxiety as central for women. That the very *looking* may be dangerous (the X-ray machine) demonstrates that looking has taken on the familiar dangers of infantile sexuality, to be sure, but again to focus only on the dangers of looking does injustice to her attempt to master her anxiety. Her need to see and know what is inside must be dealt with as positive and adaptive; this woman suffers from feeling insufficiently in control. She often complains (in this session too) that her brain melts and she cannot keep ideas straight. Being able to see and identify is an important element of mastery.

The following week, this same patient presented another dream, this one illustrating the need for control over access.

> I had one of my house dreams [these were varied]. There is a big old fashioned kind of Victorian house with windows all around — like a porch — not like Joe's father's — modern and sleek. I am worried about getting locks, it's so open all around. Then I get the locks and somehow you have to put the locks in a fruit, it turns into a puddle, a muddy dirty puddle.

Here the beautiful house is in danger as a result of its lovely, gracious openness. Anxiety over being able to secure entry (the lock) appears (the house is not like the man's). The genital reference is made clear by the fruit, which she describes as very soft and juicy. The fruit turns into the dirty, muddy hole, that is, the genital is experienced in anal imagery, but that is where the lock is in this patient's dream, where the sphincter has control.

The confusion of anal and genital has long been noted in analytic literature; the vagina is often experienced as dirty, due to the internal location that easily leads to equating the vagina with the rectum. The confusion is reinforced by the diffusion of sensation, amply demonstrated by cloacal theories of childbirth. While all of this is familiar to us, what I wish to introduce as an additional and important factor for the female is that the anal sphere is one in which the female has been able to demonstrate control. It therefore carries the meaning of power, which, in boys, is distributed between the anal component and the phallic one.

While girls have long been described as neater, cleaner, and more easily toilet trained, I am proposing that an independent source of this development derives spontaneously from the girl's need to master and integrate genital anxieties, that the internal nature of the genital connects with anality, and genital excitement redoubles her need to exercise control. This occurs independently from influences of the relationship with her mother.

INHERENT CONFLICTS

In the preceding discussion of what I consider to be typically female efforts at mastery of genital anxieties, I did not elaborate the inherent conflicts involved in each attempt at mastery. It is essential to realize that these efforts are not simple, harmonious experiences. One predominant element, the reliance on the mother, is occurring within a relationship fraught with difficulties inherent in the age. A relationship of trust is essential; the girl must rely on her mother's reassurance that her genital is, indeed, inside (Keiser 1953). "Seeing is believing" gives concrete reality to boys' definition, whereas a girl must integrate her genital on a sense of faith; she must "know" it without evidence and must trust her mother's explanation.[3]

The girl's need for her mother to help her master her genital anxieties occurs during the same period in which the natural thrust of development calls for a turn away from her in the service of the task of separation–individuation. Viewed from a libidinal perspective, this is the period in which children are struggling for control over their own bodies and often are engaged in a power struggle with their mothers. Two of the specific genital anxieties repeat and intensify anxieties already inherent in developmental conflicts. The turn to mother threatens reengulfment, requires a "yes" (I am like you) when autonomous strivings require a "no." Hence, the ambivalence and intensity of battles between mother and daughter, the clinging and fighting, are fueled from multiple sources long before rivalry for father is an issue.

Not only must the little girl turn to her mother in her mastery efforts, she also must, like the little boy with his father, form an identification with her as a female. Kleeman (1976) has pointed out the importance that role labeling

---

[3]Proprioceptive and vascular sensations occur spontaneously but can be either repressed or integrated: parental support is critical for integration to occur.

plays in organizing the child's gender identity, and language begins to play a major role in organizing the world during this same period. This very organizing function, that of being female like mother, important for the integration of genital and gender experiences, threatens the task of individuation, which requires being different from mother. Moreover, every identification is built upon older experiences (Reich 1954), so that the resurrection of the earliest, symbiotic primary identification and diffusivity threatens the ego's struggle for definition. This reverberation between genital anxieties and symbiotic anxieties contributes to the girl's difficulty in articulating boundaries; diffusivity and control issues are pervasive.

The interaction between control of her body and differentiation from her mother is demonstrated by a woman who dreamt of a building in which she was anxiously trying to secure the doors and window, barring entry.[4] The associations merited the interpretation that the invasion (her dream word) she feared was genital and that she was trying to secure control over genital entry. Associations to a rape during adolescence confirmed the interpretation, and the patient felt relieved of a sullen recalcitrance that had characterized her mood during several sessions. She said she really felt "understood," and left feeling lightened. She opened the following session with, "I can't give you any credit for my feeling better, you'll make it all yours," a theme often demonstrated in this treatment by chronic complaints

---

[4]In my experience, female patients of all ages dream quite frequently of anxiety about entry through doors and windows. Standard interpretation would be about sexual anxiety. I have found that interpretation of the anxiety as being over control of the opening is effective in mastery of that anxiety. It makes a big difference whether the patient's fear that she is invadable is confirmed or her wish for control is confirmed.

that mother always took over her feeling.[5] She again described her inability to have anything good because mother takes it, feeling it more than the patient herself. Associations to the recent illness of her boyfriend reiterated her blurring of boundaries in that his pain became her pain. The whole issue of psychic boundaries flowed from the anxiety about body boundaries.

While there has been a current trend, primarily in academic psychology, sociology, and among some psychoanalysts to idealize the mother–daughter tie, it does not reflect accurately the struggles that emerge in the analytic situation, where intense ambivalence seems to predominate. The longing to be one with mother and the fear thereof reflect the basic ambivalence present in the symbiotic situation and indicate both the desire for identity and the desire for differentiation. Whichever way the girl turns at this point, anxiety is generated.

Derivatives of this position seem to present themselves in adult women during pregnancy. A new genital anxiety confronts pregnant women and one hears all the infantile anxieties; women fear damage to their bodies from the forthcoming childbirth, they cannot imagine their body's participation, and they fear the pain. They feel an urgency about being close to their mothers but simultaneously push them away. They wish to merge with their forthcoming infants but often structure their lives so as to ensure not becoming immersed in the maternal experiences, as one woman put it, of "being lost in the swamp" of motherhood.

---

[5]Such problems are more acute when mothers overidentify with their children, as did this woman's mother, or are generally intrusive. Mothers seem to be in this position more frequently with their daughters than with their sons. I think the reflection from the genital to the psychic is inherent in girls, although it can be made more difficult by particular kinds of mothering.

As in early childhood, in pregnancy one witnesses all the inner confusion, the regression to other modes of control (sometimes in work, sometimes controlling husband or others by making demands), before some balance of identifications and differentiation from their own mothers is integrated with the physical experience (see also Kestenberg 1976). During pregnancy, fantasies of an internal penis are resurrected as a concretization of the unknown experience. In recent years, several women who have had ultrasound scans during their pregnancies have been delighted about the concretization given by the visual experience of seeing their fetuses. Despite all the explicit educational material available to women, the mysteriousness of what is going on inside their bodies seems to me to reflect that early, undefined mysteriousness. One woman enacted the search for concretization by looking closely into the mirror and finding, that if she looked closely, she could "see" something of her genital. Another revealed the use of a pen for masturbation, describing the need and pleasure in defining her genital experience.

In a case presented to illustrate some of the developing girl's difficulties, Silverman (1981) illustrates the confluence of anxieties.

Faith demonstrates the symbolic use of the penis as an instrument of control over what can come out of her body. If she had one of those, she could see, touch, and, although not manifestly stated, show her "overalls." The little girl, Faith, had a boot fetish (worn whenever she left home) and, when excited, wet herself. At age 6½ she was insufficiently differentiated from her mother so that she was unable to attend nursery school.

Analysis of the fetish revealed two components. Boots was the name of a cat "whom mother continually threatened to send away because periodically it went round the house spraying the furniture. . . . living in terror that she herself would be sent away for her own wetting, Faith had contrived to keep Boots with her in one form or other at all times" (p. 591).

Recalling her wetting led to the second insight. "She had watched her mother watering the garden and had seen that she *controlled* the stream with something, the nozzle, that very much resembled her brother's penis. If only she had had one of those, she told me, she would have been able to *control* her urinary stream and would have been able to avoid all her consternation and misery" (p. 591, italics added). Silverman interprets this material as an example of penis envy and genital confusion. After considerable work in this direction, Silverman made the interpretation to Faith that she wanted what her brother Frank had. Again I quote: " 'That's right!' she shouted, and she pounded the table with her fist. 'I want my overalls *outside* like he has. He can *see* his overalls. He can *touch* his overalls. I can't see mine, I can't touch mine. *I don't know myself.*' The fetish was given up, never to be resumed" (p. 592).

I find this case an extraordinary example of the girl's preoccupations. Her needs to have access, to concretize, to control and to retain her object are all expressed in the boots. Here penis envy is clearly metaphor (Grossman and Stewart 1976) for her own concerns over mastery through sensory modes and demonstrates the interaction between body integrity and the developmental task of individuation. While Silverman does not elaborate, we can assume that the relinquishing of the fetish was accompanied by an increment in psychic individuation and that Faith became more capable of leaving her own mother as a result. Some resolution of conflicts over mastering her own body diminished anxiety and enabled her to relinquish dependency on an object (Boots/mother/penis), that is, to effect separation. Her anxiety over genitals that were beyond voluntary sensory control kept her dependently clinging to her mother.

Mastery over the body is a central issue as toddlers attempt individuation and autonomy. The issues I have been describing seem to be central for little girls. While the separation-individuation struggle is predominantly an issue between the girl and her mother, fathers play a significant role that has been underestimated. Fathers have not been seen as significant in the first two years of life; they seem to appear as "knights in shining armor" in the toddler phase and become fully important only during the oedipal phase.

Recent research finds that infants particularly like the father's low voice at 28 weeks; Mohaczy (1968; cited in Abelin 1971) found a mild stranger reaction only where the fathers were not actively interacting with their infants. Abelin (1971) found precursors of attachments to fathers very early; all but one of the infants studied recognized the father with a happy smile before 6 months and all were firmly attached to their fathers by 9 months. The girls he observed attached themselves earlier and more intensely than boys did.

In Abelin's studies, during the toddler phase, most relevant to this discussion, toddlers' relationships with their fathers were markedly different from those with their mothers. The relationships with fathers were filled with "wild exuberance"; fathers appeared a "stable island," while mothers were ambivalently cathected. Fathers were not experienced as rivals at a time when other children were experienced as rivals for mother's attention. A few weeks following the rapprochement crisis, father images were evoked in play, stories, and pictures when children were distressed with their mothers. Abelin suggests the resolution of the separation-individuation struggle might be impossible for both mother and child without having father to turn to. Brooks's and Lewis's (1979) findings that 15-month-olds were able to identify their fathers from a picture, but none was able to identify the mother, stresses the importance of difference in the forming of articulated images.

Chasseguet-Smirgel (1970) has recognized the importance

of fathers to girls in their attempts to separate from their mothers. Viewing the struggle as saturated with aggression, fathers emerge as those with power over mother. In fantasy, the girl seizes the father's penis to find power against her image of the angry, controlling mother (created by the projection of her own rage), and subsequently the tie to her father is colored by her guilt toward him for having castrated him. The research on early development I described above suggests the existence of a more benign relationship with her father (the stable island). The father as a reliable resource is as important, if not more so, to girls as he is to boys, since girls must rely more than boys do on others to effect separation. Since her own anatomy cannot help her, the girl's mastery requires a turn to objects for both support and identifications. At this early stage, these object relationships seem to be relatively nonconflictual for children of both genders; I wish to stress the ongoing object embeddedness in the girl's development.

Vignettes from a two-year period of an analysis illustrate the interaction between mastering female genital anxieties and individuation, and the reliance on others to achieve this. Miss C. dreamed she was in her bedroom and there were two heavy doors to give her safety, but high above was a small open transom window she could not lock, leaving her vulnerable. This imagery, which I discussed earlier, is always expressive of multiple anxieties including genital ones. In this case the genital anxieties of access and penetration, and relationship issues involving an intrusive mother and domineering powerful men converge in the attempt to achieve individuation. The patient's associations at this time led her to never having privacy or being able to make her own decisions, and to her cultural world in which men indeed had all the power and women were expected peaceably to submit to all their wishes, including sexuality. To interpret solely along the lines of her fear and helplessness about someone entering would not be helpful because the issues involved individuation and autonomy as well. Note that in this dream the patient is quite alone, the only condition in which she has any measure of safety.

During the subsequent two years of analytic work, several themes were developed. One of the prominent ones was what I have called in Chapter 2 a "forbidden identification" with the powerful grandfather who lived in and dominated her childhood home. This forbidden identification deprived her of a satisfactory route out of the immersion with her mother and the preparatory familiarity (Glover and Mendell 1982) that would help her into a comfortable relationship with men. Some work on her fear of this unconscious identification led to the transference dream that *she was driving her doctor's car around, having a wonderful time, although somewhat anxious that she did not have permission to take it.* This anxiety reflects both the forbidden identification and Chasseguet-Smirgel's (1970) description of a guilt-ridden usurpation of the father's power.

The next dream that took place in that same room illustrated her fear of being overwhelmed not only by a man but by her own powerful sexual impulses; she dreamed that *the ceiling was wide open and everything could come pouring in.* The door, as image, reappeared following some interest in an appropriate man during the analyst's vacation: "A man is trying to get in the door; it is not locked. I turn to this woman in a rage, screaming 'Why are you not helping me?' " A proper rage at her own mother, whose passivity in all things left my patient unaided in her feminine development, was now alive in the transference. As work progressed along these lines of interpretation, the patient dreamed that she was trying to get from one floor to another on an elevator, but there was no control panel. She finally found a cleaning woman who helped her. Association led to a maid who in childhood had washed the patient's hair, and, with further exploration, to memories that she bathed her, including her genitals. My interpretation that she felt she had no control panel but had to rely on others to master her body experiences finally led to the concretization of these anxieties in a dream in which a bicycle or motorcycle went from between her legs straight at her mother, with all the overdetermination of that image. These themes in this patient's analysis illustrate several of the issues under discussion: the need to feel in control of her own body sexually as well as in relation to others, her need for a paternal identification to precede sexual involvement, and the need for her mother to support her in her sexuality. The wish to control her own body (space) carries both referents of psychic autonomy and body integrity.

There are implications for psychoanalytic and psychotherapeutic technique that have been implicitly suggested in the material that I have presented; here I would like to make them explicit. Viewing female anxieties as unique leads to a variety of issues central to the developing self. The girl's genital anxieties parallel other anxieties characteristic of the early stages of development. One of the most important mechanisms available to her is that of identification, itself a natural mode for both girls and boys in mastering the developmental conflicts of the age. Turning to her mother to help her master anxiety, she is faced with anxiety emanating from the very identification she needs to consolidate. Anxiety rises from conflicts over regression versus progression, identification versus differentiation, dependency versus autonomy, and control versus helplessness. Unlike identifications with father, for both boys and girls, the identifications with mother are dangerous because of the early relationship that is resurrected when the more advanced identifications are being made.

If one interprets the conflicts in these terms, women will find sources for mastering their anxiety and resolving their conflicts, a far different aim from that of helping them "accept" a castrated state and settle for substitutes. Female resolution may lead to a wider range of solutions than we are accustomed to seeing in the male; one patient reached control over anality (money and entry, as she will decide who can sit in the seat she owns); Ms. A. will "sink her teeth" gleefully into many of life's problems and intellectual pursuits without feeling like a fraud; another patient has taken control of her own pleasures, sexual as well as others. All girls must find a way of resolving the anxiety aroused by the necessary identifications with the mother on whom they must rely far more than is necessary for boys. This object embeddedness has long been considered the hallmark of feminine character (Gilligan 1983).

GENITAL ANXIETIES AND OBJECT RELATIONSHIPS

I have tried to illustrate that girls' genital anxieties derive from the characteristics of the female genitalia and to identify some of these anxieties. Her fears, anxieties, and psychic fantasies must be explored in relation to her own body in the same way that castration anxiety, phallic preoccupation, and fantasy must be elaborated for boys. As the nature of the genitals and genital anxieties are different, of necessity, the mechanisms for mastering them differ also.

Here I have identified three interrelated anxieties: access, penetration, and diffusivity. I am suggesting that the girl's experience with the unfocused, open, penetrable nature of her genital creates difficulties in forming mental representations of her body that have clear boundaries and sharp definition. Further, I suggest that this unfocused representation of the genitals complicates the formation of ego boundaries and a firm sense of self, and contributes to both the mental and body issues of which women complain; they describe mental "fuzziness" in trying to think, and complain of fluid body images (Lerner 1976).

Attempts at mastery include externalization, concretization, regression, and, most unique to the girl, a greater reliance on others than for boys. She must rely on trust, dependency, and identification with mother's body, quite different from the boy's direct sensory experience, which is visual, tactile, and can be confirmed by manipulation. This, in turn, contributes to the object embeddedness of the girl's existence, so long an observed female characteristic.

The timetable for integrating gender and the body into the emerging self is complicated because she must turn to her mother at the time that development of autonomy requires a turn away from her. Critical identifications with her father are as important to the girl at this stage as they have always been considered to be for boys. Fathers have a dual role at this point; the girl requires both his affirmation of her femininity and his welcoming identifications with him.

While the girl's oedipal phase will be discussed more fully in Chapter 5, I would like to suggest that the fantasies at this time are an overlay of the earlier ones and the preferred modes of mastery again appear. If the girl has been able to integrate her early genital anxieties, identify with her mother, be at one with her in her femaleness and, simultaneously, identify with a father who sees her as female but facilitates identification with him, thus securing her difference from her mother, then she is developmentally in a position to enter the fraught rivalrous nature of the oedipal, bear the fears and disappointments of that phase, and arrive at true genitality.

4

The Female Superego:
A Different Perspective

TOWARD A PERSPECTIVE ON THE
GENDER-SPECIFIC SUPEREGO

Freud's theories concerning the development of the superego in women reflect his theories about female development as a whole, that is, all female development is seen as a variation of male development. While he hinted that female development might be different in the preoedipal years (Freud 1933), and suggested that female analysts would need to elucidate female psychology, at no time did he envision feminine development as a unique process that gives rise to a different character, different identity formation, and, necessarily, a different superego. This is dramatically illustrated by his statement, "The male sex seems to have taken the lead in all these moral acquisitions: and they seem to have been transmitted to women by cross-inheritance" (Freud 1923, p. 37).

The presumption of identical development in boys and girls is not exclusively Freud's. A massive amount of observational data has accumulated about differences between male and female children (well summarized by Barglow and Schaefer 1976). We know, from studies in various fields, that boy and girl babies are held differently, and with different frequency, that they are talked to differently, given different toys, reacted to in different ways; we know that their body experiences differ; we know that motoric development differs; and we know that gender identity is firmly established by about 24 months of age (Stoller 1968). All of this knowledge has not been well integrated into our theory, although it enters our clinical work. Discussions of symbiosis, separation-individuation, rapprochement, all proceed as though they are occurring in precisely the same psyche. I believe this is the heritage of Freud's early formulation that the little girl is a "little man" (Freud 1933) until the phallic crisis, and that development is identical for boys and girls until that time.

Freud's (1925) statement about the female superego is worth examining: "Their superego is never so inexorable, so impersonal, so independent of its emotional origins as we require it to be in men" (p. 257). This formulation has led to the generalization that the female superego is weaker, a hypothesis that decades of clinical work has not confirmed. All analysts can testify to the strength and inflexibility of the feminine superego, its relentlessness in certain areas. For instance, all of us have worked with women whose sexuality, despite currently changed external mores, remains frozen, unexpressed, frightening—under early prohibitions. At the same time, Freud's statement clearly contains his own observations of differences in the male and female superegos, although he did not elaborate what he meant by "so impersonal and so independent of its origins."

The differences Freud noted are reflected in art and myths. Justice is portrayed as a woman. She stands calmly, blindfolded, holding scales in her hands. The symbols of the blindfold and scales are pertinent to my thesis. As manifest content, the scales symbolize the measuring of evidence; the blindfold symbolizes impartiality. Latently, the image implies an internal orientation, a sensing, weighing, and balancing quality. This image is in marked contrast to that of Moses, who sits staring outward with the stone tablets of the Ten Commandments in his hands.

It is indeed ironic that Justice, portrayed as a woman, sits over courts of justice in much of the world, while psychoanalytic theory portrays women with defective superegos. The very moods of these two images express differences deeply felt throughout history in these concrete projections of male and female superegos. Indeed, even during Freud's era, women were the keepers of morality, while men had two roles. On the one hand, they set the standards; on the other, they were allowed far more violations than would have been tolerated in women. What were "wild oats" to a young man would have made a "fallen woman" of a young girl.

I can define two issues that contribute to this inconsistency. First, Freud selected a quality that is more characteristic of men and used it as the criteria for desirable superego development; that quality is *firmer* structure, a quality that may or may not be more desirable than the more *flexible* structure that is more characteristic of women. In the film *The Bridge on the River Kwai,* the Major found himself on the brink of treason, building a fine bridge for the enemy, following the rigidly fixed superego commandment, "Do your job the very best you can." The firm structure and the inexorable nature of the superego did not lead to a moral decision. I do think that law is a masculine achievement (Mosaic), but law cannot be equated with ethics or morality.

While I cannot deal here with ethics and morality (ironic as that is in a discussion of the superego), it is clear that

Freud's criteria for desirable superego development is inadequate. The organizers that I propose for the study of the
superego are structure, strength, and contents. I believe these
aspects (or axes) can provide a framework in which issues of
morality, ethics, law, as well as other superego aspects can be
examined.[1]

A second source of the difficulty in Freud's formulation
results from his insistence on the centrality of the Oedipus
complex and inherent conflicts as the motivating force for
developing a superego. First, placing the motivation for
superego development in the midst of the phallic-oedipal
phase gives undue importance to castration anxiety. The
harshness and exactingness of the male superego is attributed
to the rages and fears arising from castration anxiety generated by phallic-oedipal impulses. "Castration" having already taken place and propelled girls into the oedipal phase,
they do not have the motivation for superego development
that boys do, nor do their superegos bear the same harshness
(as I have noted, there is no evidence for this assertion).

A second complication that results from setting the stage
for superego development at this late period is that the
superego is more likely to be influenced by developmental
processes characteristic of that period.[2] If the core of the

---

[1]In his discussion of this paper, of which I am very appreciative, Dr.
Roy Schafer suggested the word *axes* for these categories; there could, of
course, be many such axes along which different aspects of the superego
could be examined and perhaps quantified. For instance, *function* would
be another axis. I think the term a particularly good one because it allows
us to conceptualize measurement of any number of different topics.

[2]Chassel (1967) suggests that Freud observed developmental incre-
ments in ego and superego development at the time of oedipal resolution
and attributed a causal connection to issues that were only temporally
related.

superego is, though, established much earlier, the core must remain tied to earlier processes and introjections. It must bear the irrationality, the projections, of the earlier period — primitive qualities characteristic of most superegos. The organization into the superego as a structure that occurs at the oedipal period is subject to later influences. These influences include greater cognitive capacities, better reality testing, advanced sexual identifications,[3] the ongoing experience of the body, the cultural contributions that affect the selection and expression of desirable qualities for both sexes. All of these factors differ for boys and girls, since their life experiences have differed from birth onward. Greenacre (1952) has called the body "its own environment" (p. 149). This, together with the input from the outer world as conveyed to the child through the physical and emotional communications from its parents, creates different worlds in which boys and girls live long before the time of oedipal superego organization. It is not only the phallic phase that is different; development has been different from the moment of birth.

Generally, preoedipal manifestations of a superego have been called *precursors*. Webster defines a precursor as a "harbinger," a guide to what is to follow. In referring to preoedipal components as precursors, their importance is diminished more than seems justifiable. It is my impression that the early irrational core of the superego remains dominant in the superegos of both boys and girls, and largely determines the ego and superego identifications that are

---

[3]Fast (1979) elaborates the significance of the differences between primitive and advanced sexual identifications. For a comprehensive discussion of identification as an aspect of internalization, see Schafer (1968).

made through the first years of life, through the separation-individuation phases, and forms the basis for the critical phallic-oedipal identifications (Sandler 1960).

Many have observed that little girls are more obedient than boys, more easily toilet trained, and more compliant. These qualities indicate quite early prohibitions that I would see as evidence of superego formation, in that there are clear internalizations prohibiting and shaping drive expression. The boy's core identifications (both ego and superego) undergo more changes because the earliest object of identification, the mother, must be transformed into the father (Loewald 1979). This necessary transformation places stresses on boys that give rise to anxieties and instability, in addition to castration anxiety, all of which affect the structuralization that takes place at the oedipal period.

Exploring differences between the male and female superego is complicated by the fact that in discussions of the superego, very different concepts are joined indiscriminately. Words like "harshness," "strength," "rigidity," "weakness," "prohibitions," "ideals," and, occasionally, "kindness," all refer to very different aspects of the superego, and there is much work to be done in organizing these disparate concepts (see Hartmann 1960, Sandler 1960, Schafer 1960 for discussions of some of these issues). Each of these has a different history in preoedipal development; some, I think, are universally different in the male and female.

THE ATTRIBUTES OF THE SUPEREGO: STRENGTH, CONTENTS, AND STRUCTURE

Here I will try to define and trace the history of three aspects of the superego, the strength, the structure, and the contents (see also Applegarth 1976, Blum 1976, and Chapter 2 of this book). There is confusion between the superego as a structure, the contents of the structure, and the strength of that structure. It is necessary to explore these in order to determine whether there are differences between male and female superegos, and if so, what these differences are.

Contents refers to the specific admonitions and prohibitions—which drives are allowed expression, in which ways drives may be expressed, which are prohibited. Some contents seem universal, such as the incest taboo; others are culturally dependent. There have been many observations of the strict codes of idiosyncratic ethics among criminal subgroups. While Mafia members can and must rob and murder, the group is known for strong family ties, loyalty, and protection of children. In various religions, we can see another example of differences in content: one religion prohibits suicide, another idealizes, even demands it. The contents of the superego contain both ideals and taboos. Members of each group clearly have superegos, although one group may appear immoral (lacking a superego) to members of other groups whose superegos have different contents. Then too, as we know, many superego activities have little to do with morality although they are experienced as greatly important. Trivia may assume heroic proportions of "right" and "wrong."

Strength refers to the efficiency with which the contents are regulated. Superego strength should not be measured by the nature of its contents (which is commonly done) but by how powerfully the contents are enforced. For example, the content "be pliant," or "be obedient," can create a pliant person who appears to have a "weak" superego (Blum 1976), that is, one who appears to lack his or her own standards. In fact, it may take much strength to enforce that directive. All of us have encountered individuals who describe themselves as having been quite independent, assertive, even rebellious, as young children until "something came over" them. They complain of their adult passivity, obedience to and fear of authority, in contrast to their early, energetic, impish childhoods.

Structure refers to the organization, or interrelationship of the contents; the contents can have different strengths. For example, given two contents, "I should prepare dinner for my children" and "I should work for a professional paper," male and female responses would be very different. Men, in Western culture, would have no conflict in this area; the commitment to work is fixed, dominant, and supersedes most other contents. Men may have conflicts that impinge on their working but *that* they should work is without question, that is, a fixed content. For women, the relative strengths of the two contents are not so fixed, but vary according to the situation. Women are more likely to experience conflict in choosing which of the contents will be given dominance, and they are far more likely to experience guilt (no matter what their choice). It is my opinion that the organization of contents, that is, the structure, is far more fixed in men, more flexible in women, due to developmental factors that I will later elaborate.

It is possible to have a superego with rigid structure, many contents, enforced with great strength that could produce an "immoral" decision. It is also possible that a variation in either the content, rigidity of the structure, or the strength could completely change the decision from an "immoral" one to a "moral" one. For example, had the Major in *Bridge on the River Kwai* a less rigid structure, he could have substituted the content of patriotism and so acted in such a way as to be considered moral.

Freud, in support of his hypothesis that women's superegos were less inexorable than men's, described women whose mores and standards changed to conform with those of their lovers, hence a "weaker" superego. To reformulate this in terms of this discussion, one would say that the contents of these women's superegos contained directives to be obedient and follow the standards set down by the men with whom they were allied. I think that, in a reflexive way, the contents of the feminine superego affect the structure, commanding as it were, that it should not be independent, that is, not retain or assert its own hierarchy. Thus, traditional values, or contents, for women affect structure in determining which identifications (ego and superego) can be made and which are forbidden. This further affects the structure of the superego as it is revised throughout life, continually influencing the relative strength of specific superego contents.

Women's assertiveness training groups, which have become so popular, do two things. First, they are giving active encouragement to assertive behavior that has been traditionally forbidden women except in special circumstances. When aggression is expressed on behalf of the protection of their children or their homes, it is approved. In every other circumstance, "aggressive" as an attribute of a woman is pejorative. Clinically, we note that tremendous anxiety emerges when aggressive fantasies are touched on, or aggressive behavior stimulated.

The second relevant aspect of these groups has not been given recognition but is of great importance to us as analysts, not only for clinical relevance but for what it may reveal of women's superegos. The external groups are taking on the function of early parental and social groups and, inherent in their title, give permission to women to *be* assertive. Much like Freud's description of the Church and the Army (1921), a superego function (internal) is reexternalized and reinternalized with new content. This covert aspect may be the most important function of these groups, as, in the process, the anxiety level that women have traditionally experienced over expressing aggression is reduced.

The above gives a contemporary example of a desirable quality I am calling *flexibility* within the female superego. There is a distortion of Freud's observation that women's superego is "never so inexorable" as men's that has led to interpreting this to mean weak and defective. Weakness, however, refers to the power and efficiency with which drives are controlled, and weakness would imply a failure of control. Such failure would be expressed in breakthroughs of drive, failure to conform to the prohibitions or directives (contents). There is no evidence that this is the case more with women than with men.

Quite the contrary seems to be true; rather than permit occasional defiance of superego strictures, women seem to repress massively, often to somaticize, be "nervous." In analyses, when instinctual material is emerging, I have found that women are loath to admit to the material, or to express it, even when it is clear in dreams and in associations. They seem unable to enjoy elaborate fantasies to anywhere near the degree that men do. Given the emergence in analysis of sexual or aggressive impulses, I have rather consistently found men more ready to elaborate grand fantasies of pleasure, sensuality, and conquest than are women with the same instinctual material emerging.[4] Men have repeatedly elaborated James Bond-like fantasies of sexual prowess, Walter Mitty-type fantasies of heroism and success. When associations point to longings for stardom and fame, admi-

---

[4]I had asked two colleagues to read an early draft of this chapter. One noted here, "This is certainly true, but only as regards sexuality." The other noted, "This is certainly true, but only as regards aggression."

ration and power, women are ashamed, timid, and anxious. This is reflected and powerfully reinforced culturally, as movies, novels, and pornography are primarily oriented around male fantasy. There seems to be far greater, not less, control exercised by women's superegos of the expression of the forbidden; more, not less, effective restriction and inhibition.

Many authors (Greenacre 1952, Jacobson 1964, Kestenberg 1968) have noted that little girls are more easily socialized, cleaner and neater, more obedient earlier than boys. Greenacre found women to have a "fund of guilt." Following Freud in attributing a central position to castration in the formation of the superego, Greenacre reversed Freud's conclusions. She hypothesized that the girl, finding herself castrated, assumed her castration was a punishment inflicted on her because of her masturbation. As a result, girls have a greater struggle against their sexuality (see also Jacobson 1964) and an "enormous enhancement of later guilt feelings in situations of conflict." She found marked "diffuse or aimless conscientiousness" and differentiated it: "Such conscientiousness . . . is to be distinguished from firmer, more condensed conscience structure more characteristic of the male" (p. 159).

GENDER ASSIGNMENT
AND BODY EXPERIENCE

I am going to explore these observed differences between male and female superegos by examining some aspects of gender. The first area will be gender assignment; the second, the experience of the physical differences; the third, the impact of gender on identifications.

Gender Assignment

The very first thing asked upon the birth of a newborn baby is not the size or weight or health, but its gender, "A boy or a girl?" Long before birth, the newborn is the object of elaborate fantasies for both parents. The first communication to the infant surely includes whether that child is a fulfillment or disappointment of its parents' dreams. Along with the assignment of gender come a multitude of expectations and messages that are expressed to the child in many ways—in how and how often it is talked to, cooed at, the toys it is given, whether activity is encouraged or discouraged, whether flirtatiousness is found charming or unattractive. Much of this treatment reflects the stereotyped expectations for boys' and girls' behavior; often it affirms the natural inclination of the child; often it is counter to the child's individual nature. It always conveys messages as to what are expected and desirable responses; all of these messages weave their way into the contents of the superego as well as the formation of the ego. So powerful is gender assignment that it can result in irreversible genetically incorrect gender identity. Stoller (1968) has documented cases in which, because of anatomic aberrations, incorrect gender assignment has been made and led to irreversible experiences of gender identity due to the impact of the child–parent interaction.

Stoller's findings, along with those of Kestenberg (1956a), Galenson and Roiphe (1976), and, more recently, Frankel and Sherick (1979), give support based on developmental observations to Jones's (1927, 1947) and Horney's (1924) assertions that feminine identity is primary and firmly established long before the phallic phase, most likely between 18 and 24 months, in the midst of separation-individuation struggles.

The specific messages communicated to children, while conveying sociocultural expectations for boys and girls, also include each individual mother's unique personal message. These latter will vary with each mother's own history and the meaning of each child at the specific point in her life (for instance, a first son, or a third daughter).

Over and beyond all these collective and individual communications, there is one difference every mother experiences with her boy and girl baby, that is, the child's gender in relation to her own. I propose that the mother's experience of the girl as like herself, and the boy as different from herself, ties the girl to the mother in a reciprocal relationship and orients the boy to differentiate, from birth onward. In the body of her infant daughter, a mother can see her own past self; the body is known and familiar, one with which she can have total identification. In contrast, a boy can only be experienced by a woman as different from herself; there cannot be the deep biological understanding of the male body experience that a woman has with her daughter's. The mother's experience of her daughter as like herself, and her experience of her son as different, is overtly and subtly communicated to her children. The girl early experiences sameness (see Schafer 1968); the boy, difference.

The earliest stage of mental life is characterized by diffusion, lack of differentiation between outer and inner, between self and mother. The girl's sameness reflected back to her by mother's mirroring, reinforces the blurring of self boundaries, and self and object boundaries. It begins a process that is repeated in different ways throughout each stage and aspect of development, culminating in many differences in the egos and superegos of boys and girls. One of the most common complaints of women in treatment is that their mothers "never saw" them. "I don't think she ever saw me"; "I didn't come into focus for her"; "She always expected me to like what she likes, and is surprised and upset if I differ"; "She expected me to grow up to be exactly like her"; "She dressed me in the colors that she looked well in." The list is endless, the influence pervasive.

The Body Experience

Simultaneously with the internalization of the mother's mirroring, the child's body experience is making its contribution to the development of self representations. While we are accustomed to saying that the ego is at core a "body ego," discussions of the ego then proceed without noting the influence of genital experiences. Greenacre (1952), in calling the anatomy the "primary environment," does not give sufficient recognition to the powerful influence of gender assignment. On one hand, discussions of the developing psyche omit body experience (Hartmann 1960, Mahler 1974); on the other, the focus is totally on the body (Deutsch 1944, Freud 1931, Jacobson 1964). These effects seem complementary and mutually reinforcing, and deserve a great deal of study.

Many authors have noted the different genital experiences of boys and girls (Erikson 1964, Greenacre 1952, Jacobson 1964, Kestenberg 1956a, 1968). The differences are many. The penis can be seen and felt; one can act on it and with it. The penis provides boys with a visible, concrete location for their excitation, a specific physical presence for an intense experience. The boy's sexual experience with its boundaried specificity leads to clearly focused, defined visible boundaries of his own body; this translates into a clear mental image. In contrast, the girl's experience is internal, diffuse, generalized. The girl cannot see her genitals, she cannot locate visually the source of her pleasure. Touching the external genitals (clitoris) stimulates the internal (vaginal); the internal stimulates the anal.

There is an additional element that seems relevant but has been undervalued, that is, the use of the hands. In addition to the genital sensations, boys can define, manipulate, stimulate the genitals with their hands (for masturbatory differences, see Clower 1976). The hands define the contours, the size, shape, and specific areas of heightened pleasure. There are three sensory sources for the developing body image: the visual, sensations in the genital area, and the tactile sensations in the hands and fingers.

This defining body experience is different for the girl in the midst of the same psychic development. Her eyes, her hands, her genitals, do not provide clearly defined boundaries. In attempting to form a mental image of herself and her experiences, she repeats, from within her own body, the nonspecific, generalized, undifferentiated psychic experience of earlier stages.[5]

The boy's sexual experience with its boundaried specificity opposes the undifferentiated symbiotic experience. In addition, the penis is eminently suited to support the individuation process since, when there is excitement, it serves as a natural anatomical vehicle for the drive outward (discharge).

In times of excitement, the girl's body experience leads her inward and back to a more diffuse, undifferentiated state. Basic psychic differences between male and female are established from within their own bodies. Female intuition, as a major mode of approaching a problem, has long been observed, in contrast to male "clear" cognition. (Do women think from the inside out, men from the outside in?) Witkin's (1962) studies, which found women "field dependent" and

---

[5]All the homunculi pictured in psychology textbooks are of men. It would be informative to have such physiologic mental maps of women.

global, and men "field independent" and analytic, seem to point to cognitive styles that reflect these earliest building blocks of cognition.

Anatomy, influencing the experience and imaging of the body, plays this important role in the individuation process; this is expressed in our clinical material but usually attributed to penis envy. What women say is not "I want a penis." Usually it's "Men can go out in the world," "Men can travel," "Men leave home," "Everyone expects men to be independent." Commonly, these are understood to be manifestations of penis envy. If we consider these complaints as manifest content, then the latent content is surely, "Men can separate, individuate, become separate human beings"; women often are not able to achieve this degree of autonomy, nor is it expected of them.

Early, Abraham (1920) suggested that penis envy was related to "oral" envy. More recently, Grossman and Stewart (1976) have suggested that penis envy, instead of "bedrock," is a metaphor for envy stemming from much earlier experiences, most probably early oral (Kleinian) envy. Fast (1979) has proposed that penis envy is not at core penis envy, but a wish to hold onto an undifferentiated state in which narcissistic grandeur could be fulfilled. These formulations, while focusing more on envy or the longing for grandiosity than separation problems, are in agreement with my impression that it is the early, undifferentiated state with mother that is at issue, not the physical organ alone. In a civilization such as ours, in which autonomy is a major criteria for maturity and self-esteem, these differences are magnified.

Here, then, is where I would place Freud's "Anatomy is destiny" (1924, p. 178). The mother's perception of the girl's anatomy and the power of gender assignment, together with the girl's own early diffuse genital experience, impede individuation. The blurred boundary between self and mother in early infancy is reflected and reinforced by her anatomy, or the impact of her anatomy on the mother's experience of her is reinforced as her body experience becomes articulated.

Psychoanalysis has been attacked for the phallocentricity of its theory; it is, however, only a reflection of values shared in almost every known culture. Many reasons have been offered to explain the veneration of the male — his strength, size, his ability to overpower the threatening omnipotent mother (Chasseguet-Smirgel 1979, Schafer 1978). The issue of psychic individuation, separation from the omnipotent, merging mother of early infancy, seems to provide a universal sphere of reference. The function of the penis as an aid in individuation may well be one additional source of this universal phallocentricity.

Penis Envy

Female identity, feminine narcissism, motivation for and the nature of the superego, fear of bodily harm — all have been attributed to penis envy and feelings of castration emerging during the phallic-oedipal phase. We now know that gender identity and anatomy have confirmed "femaleness" long before the phallic phase; indeed, Parens and colleagues (1976) propose an alternate term, the *protogenital* phase. Freud's formulation that "girls, having been castrated, therefore have nothing to fear" is not borne out in reality. Women are far more fearful of bodily harm, and men are the braver, the protectors. Women's fearfulness is usually interpreted as an expression of their castration fear. This reflects the genital focus characteristic of men — it is the boy's high evaluation of the penis that makes it so vulnerable (or perhaps its vulnerability as an external organ heightens his concern and its value). Women's fears are more generalized and seem to have to do with male size and musculature — that is, their fear of being overpowered — and, with the real understanding, along with the distortions arising from fantasies, of sexual penetration, pregnancy, and childbirth.

Although the phallic phase is not the source of either gender identity or the superego, developments during the phase make significant contributions to the structure of the superego. The intense sexual excitement of the period reawakens and reinforces the psychic experiences of the separation-individuation phase (see Galenson and Roiphe 1976, who have proposed an early genital phase). The early experiences are heightened as the sexual pleasure and meaning of the body sensations crystallize into mental images. As a little girl can now understand the meaning of penetration, the boy understands that he is the "penetrator"; her body softens as his hardens, over and over reinforcing feminine diffusion and masculine concentration. The boy's ability to direct and control his urine, to write his name in the snow, to exhibit his erect penis, to fantasize its sexual function, all continue to build the experience of a self able to operate on the outer world, and his penis becomes for him the vehicle of action.

The girl's sexual excitement, her urethral experience, her wish to exhibit and master are experienced differently. A female patient recalled sniffing the odor of urine on a bus; the odor excited her; she continued, "You know, I think I've always associated that smell with all the boys' activities, all the aggression, the play, everything that was forbidden." She continued in the next session to contrast memories of her mother, in which things were always being done *to* her — back washings, hair brushings, tickling sessions.

Nagera (1975) views the girl as deprived of an executive organ. Deprived of a mechanism for discharge (the penis), she must rely on psychic mechanisms such as identification or the creation of a fantasy phallus in order to cope. One woman, strong in many ways, anguished over "how would anyone know she was sexy or sexually aroused without anything to show." However, this is pathological, not normal.

Nagera's formulation treats the female genitals as if they are totally inert; indeed he uses the phrase "passive-feminine" to describe the goal of feminine development. Receptive is not the same as passive; there is too great a leap taken from genital receptivity to character "passivity" (Freud 1933). In reality, the vagina lubricates, sweeps, and holds the penis; or it is tight and dry, actively denying entry. The external and internal genitals give great pleasure to little girls during masturbation, as does the penis to little boys.

Chasseguet-Smirgel (1979) has described this psychoanalytic posture as "a good woman is a dead woman." The French school has focused on the role of anality in women as a defense against male domination and penetration. To deny her omnipotent power, she is to be totally controlled like the fecal mass. In this view, the woman, in spite and retaliation for being so badly treated, regresses to the grandiosity of anality and attacks the penis (and people) with the controlling sphincter. (The word "controlling" is used almost exclusively in describing women.)

In my opinion, both of these positions give too much credence to fantasy and not enough weight to the body experience. Given the powerful impulses of the phallic-oedipal period—the excitement, the urge to exhibit and to master, to compete—the girl, like the boy, evolves psychic representations based on her body experience. For her, the arousal is not only clitoral and vaginal, but naturally, anatomically, it is anal as well. The exercise of the sphincter is a natural component and need not be seen as a regression with the accompanying hostility attributed to it. It is kept more alive as an internal organ of control, and anatomically retains its associations with sexuality. During this phase of development, the boy's interest is shifted "up front" while the girl's remains inside.

Anal interests are much more subject to suppression, punishment, and shame than are urinary interests; enuresis does not evoke the reactions that bowel incontinence does. The confusion of anal and vaginal often leads to experiencing the vagina as dirty. Toilet training demands for cleanliness, prohibitions of anal exploration, inhibition of play with feces, all cast a shadow over vaginal experiences. These prohibitions of anal origin are so closely linked to the sexual, they may well be the source of greater female inhibition of sexuality, rather than presumed guilt from presumed punishment for presumed castration.

I have worked with several women in whose families this confusion was expressed in not differentiating parts of the body. The phrase "down there" was used for the entire anal-urethral-vaginal area. A woman speaking an Indian dialect assures me there is no word in the language for feminine body parts; "down there" covers it all; in contrast, there is a word for the penis.

NARCISSISM AND IDENTIFICATION

Narcissism

Female narcissism as it is expressed in clothing and jewelry is usually interpreted as a displacement from the penis, that is, girls treat their whole bodies as a penis to exhibit. Grunberger (1964) has gone so far in attributing a defensive function to feminine narcissism as to suggest that no mother can ever really value her daughter. A mother can only, unambivalently, love a son. He feels that this leaves the girl with a craving for narcissistic supplies that she then seeks perpetually to fill by seeking recognition and admiration. I do not think that feminine narcissism has as its core a defense against penis envy or maternal deprivation. (I do not mean to deny the existence of either, of course, but to challenge either as being the *source* of a universal phenomenon.)

It is my opinion that feminine narcissism has its roots in object relations, anatomy, and reality. Reality has not been popular in psychoanalytic formulations. Nevertheless, one must take into account the fact that men have opportunities for narcissistic gratification in the real world in the performance of their work or the accumulation of wealth. Until recently, admiration of their bodies has been one of the few sources of narcissistic pleasure for women.

To return to the *sources* of narcissism in women – we have been accustomed in psychoanalysis to consider the boy as the narcissistic completion of his mother. Although he may be her treasure and her prize, with all the meanings that accompany that completion (her longed for penis, etc.), his body cannot be something with which she can identify in the same way as with a girl's.

I would venture to hypothesize that part of the mother's relationship to her daughter is a reflection and resurrection (Kestenberg 1956b) of the mother's early narcissistic phase, that is, narcissism on the undifferentiated level, while the narcissism in relation to her son is a reflection of later stages of her own development – stages more characterized by object orientation (feces, penis, more differentiated object relations; see Benedek 1959). I noted this earlier in this chapter, in discussing daughters' complaints that their mothers never "saw" them outside their own sphere. This continues throughout life for women; they are defined in relation to another, usually as background (Schafer's figure-ground metaphor, 1978). A woman is first mommy's baby, then daddy's darling, then a man's wife, then someone's mommy. For women, the earliest narcissistic participation with the aggrandized mother of infancy seems a likely source of their narcissism. In addition, while the rearoused anality may cast shame on sexuality, it also contributes the overestimation characteristic of the anal phase.

These differences during the phallic-oedipal phase affect mental representations and the investment in them, which in turn affects the synthesis into ego and superego structures. The visibility of the erection, as well as urination, enables boys to evaluate their performance in an *external sphere, subject to external, measurable, standards. Size, quantity, distance, are definable and discrete.* Girls' experiences remain in and on their own bodies, unseeable and unmeasurable. The clear definition of performance gives rise to defined, measurable ego and superego representations. The lack of these external, defined, measurable experiences leaves the girl in the position of searching for the definable within and on her own body and within early relationships.

Identifications

Oedipal identifications have long been considered most crucial to the adult personality. It is their function in resolving the intense conflicts of this period that gives them their tenacity and their importance. The identifications made at this time form the character, lay down the lines for sublimation, determine future sexual objects.

Early relationships are critical in the formation of these ego and superego identifications; Annie Reich (1954) has reminded us that later identifications are based on earlier ones and bear the mark of the earlier relationships (also Ritvo and Solnit 1960). Jacobson (1964) describes early character traits as becoming ossified and culturally reinforced at the time of superego consolidation. Loewald (1979), in discussing the organization into secondary identifications in superego development, notes that the oedipal stage is still "enmeshed in and pervaded by identificatory processes" (p. 767). Freud (1923) stated, "The effects of the first identifications made in earliest childhood will be general and lasting. . . . This is apparently not in the first instance the consequence or outcome of an object-cathexis. . . . But the object-choices . . . seem normally to find their outcome in an identification of this kind, and would thus reinforce the primary one" (p. 31).

This is yet another area in which, from the beginning of life, boys' and girls' experiences differ. Boys are faced with the task of "disidentifying" (Greenson 1954) from the primary object. They are aided in this process by the role of gender assignment (discussed above); boys experience the mother's experience of them as different from themselves. Fathers aid powerfully in this process by encouraging identifications with themselves and with other men. Both parents actively discourage behavior that is directly nurturant, maternal; both actively encourage masculine activities.

Fathers offer their sons mastery of the outer world, an ally in their struggle for differentiation from the mother, and, in the sexual sphere, triumphant power over the omnipotent seeming mother of infancy. We are familiar enough with boys' clubs, later men's clubs, where no woman can ever trespass; these serve as a (continuous?) support to the separation process from mother (later, women) and at the same time offer identifications with men's activities removed from the nurturing primary atmosphere of the home.[6]

As girls are called upon to make oedipal and superego identifications, it is with the same person from whom they are trying to maintain separation and individuality. Not only are oedipal identifications difficult to make because of the conflicts arising out of fear of abandonment, rivalry, and aggression—all common to both boys and girls—but the oedipal ones are blurred by resurrected ancient identifications for girls. These critical identifications *threaten* the autonomy and individuation achieved by girls, while they serve to *reinforce* and consolidate individuation and autonomy for boys. Once again, at this later stage of development, girls are confronted with integrating characteristics of the earliest phases of life.

Freud's early focus on fathers as central figures in development has been eclipsed by almost total focus on the role of mothers for many years. Recently (Abelin 1971, Layland 1981, Loewald 1979, Ross 1979) fathers have been re-emerging in importance. This renewed focus is consonant with the importance I have found clinically in the treatment of both men and women. Most of the current literature, however, is concerned with the father–son relationship.

Analytic literature says little about the relationships of fathers and daughters. Primarily, the focus is on the father as libidinal object, as protector and rescuer from the mother. With few exceptions, fathers do not seem able to offer themselves as objects of identification to girls as they do to their sons. To the extent that the father's individuation rests

---

[6]Frankel and Sherick (1979), in studying nursery school children, found that girls "grouped" earlier and excluded boys; when asked, however, the girls reported that they had been excluded by the boys (who had not yet "grouped").

on the biological base of difference from mother, to the extent that he mobilized, or continues to mobilize the "no, I am unlike" to maintain his autonomy, the more *unable* he is to permit or welcome his daughter's identification with him as he does his son's. Repeatedly, women have complained that their fathers encouraged intellectual development and education but only up to a certain point. After years of pleasurably sharing intellectual life with their fathers (to the exclusion of their mothers), several women reported that their fathers "turned on them," accusing them of "going too far" and urging them to give up the very aspirations they had long encouraged, to become traditional wives and mothers.

Lax (1977) has documented three cases in which fathers encouraged intellectuality in their daughters, though they depreciated women. Each of these women was able to function magnificently intellectually but felt "empty" because she was cut off from the deep identification with her mother in order to acquire this welcome from her father. Menaker (1979), too, has noted this disidentification in women and has found that it functions well until such women have children, at which time it becomes maladaptive, as this disidentification (Menaker calls it *counter*-identification) prohibits the emergence of nurturant feelings and behavior.

Many analyses founder on the misinterpretation of a woman's move toward her analyst as erotic when it is often an expression of a need for identification. The following dream occurred in an analysis following a tumultuous regression into the dyadic relationship. "I appear at your office. I am dressed as a boy. I am feeling sort of sheepish, but seem to be asking you if it is okay." After some musing about homosexuality, the associations drifted to fathers who wanted their sons to follow in their footsteps, sons who wanted to be like their fathers, the patient's family's assumptions about her brother's future career and their utter lack of mention of any career for her. The patient had an acute need for her father, a physician, to recognize and encourage her professional aspirations, to permit an identification. At the same time, this identification was critical for her efforts at individuation, as every time her wish to be like her mother came up, she felt overwhelmed and feared being "swallowed up." (Other women have expressed this fear as fear of "drowning," or being caught "in the swamp" of their relationships to their mothers.) Only following the working through of this need, and her beginning to pursue a professional career, could her feminine identifications with her mother reemerge *safely* and begin to consolidate. The identification with her father (circumscribed as it, of course, must be) was a necessary acquisition that insured differentiation so that she could resurrect the early identification with her mother without "drowning" in the early symbiotic, diffuse identification with her.

This clinical impression is confirmed by a series of research studies by Silverman and colleagues (1982). In testing the therapeutic effectiveness of symbiotic fantasy, they have demonstrated sex differences in responses to symbiotic stimuli. Symbiotic fantasy provided a reliable anxiety-reducing effect in normal (as well as fairly differentiated schizophrenic) men, but not in women. The subliminal stimulus, "Mommy and I are one," provided a relief from anxiety and an increase in adaptive behavior for men. However, "My lover and I are one" (with a picture of a male and female) provided positive results for women. Silverman concluded that the sense of self is more susceptible to threat from symbiotic stimuli in women, and that it is enhanced by the fantasy of oneness with a male.

CLINICAL DOCUMENTATION

I would like to give two case examples that I think illustrate the differences in superego that I have been discussing. I think these examples contain elements of different structure, content, diffusivity/focus, in a superego response to analytic work. Both of these patients had been in treatment for several years; both exhibited strong attachments to their mothers, who felt their children should not leave them. In Miss X.'s case, the mother, a widow, had no other relationships. Mr. B.'s mother clung to him, an only child, when her husband died when Mr. B. was 5 years old. After several years of analysis for each, in which aspects of separation conflicts were worked on intensely, each was moving again toward oedipal material without the swift regressions to separation conflicts that had characterized their defenses during the early years of analytic work; each was better equipped to cope with oedipal anxieties.

Miss X. had made a major career advancement, recently redecorated her home, gone on a diet (to lose the thirty pounds she gained shortly after entering analysis with me), and was resuming an affectionate, intimate sexual relationship with an appropriate, committed professional man whom she had driven away in the second year of her analysis, out of her transference anxiety that I wanted her to be involved exclusively with me (she rationalized that she was thinking too much about him and not spending enough energy on her four-times-per-week analysis). In the midst of this burst of new (resumed) activities, she became acutely anxious and attempted the previously used route of regression, but previous analytic work blocked this path. Hence, she proceeded in a state of intense anxiety expressed in the following dream (one of several similar ones during this period): "I am walking down the street; a person, I believe it is a man, appears. We are excited to see each other and begin, as in a dream, to move toward each other, when suddenly danger appears everywhere—it seems it is behind me, between us, overhead. I feel surrounded by danger but I can't seem to know what it is, although I am straining to see or know what's going to happen. I feel very alone and scared."

Mr. B. had left his wife after a bad marriage of many years, had asked for a promotion in a job he'd held without proper recognition for ten years, had stopped visiting his mother every Saturday night and calling in between, was beginning to find that women found him attractive, and was enjoying strutting a bit like a peacock. He was beginning to wear more modern clothing that enhanced his pleasant physique, had begun to do reading and studying that enhanced his professional skills, and had begun having some satisfactory sexual experiences for the first time. Instead of presenting himself to me as a pathetic person who needed to be nurtured, he was behaving flirtatiously and seductively. At this point, he had the following dream: "I am in an elevator. There is a big box taking up a lot of space, but I jump over it to get in. I nimbly do it, but the elevator door starts to close. It's going to close on my foot, so I spin around, and as I do, it begins to close on my penis. I awaken terrified."

RECAPITULATION: THE FEMALE SUPEREGO

Strength

As I said earlier, there is no evidence that girls and women have less effective control over drives than do boys and men.

While I am in agreement that women have less castration anxiety, I do not agree that this leaves them with defective superegos. The strength of the superego in women has other sources. First, it derives from fear of, and resurrected identifications with, the omnipotent seeming mother of the earliest identification — the grandiose, narcissistic mother of infancy. The second source lies in the confusion and diffusion between genital and anal; all the prohibitions of the anal impulses and conflicts cast a shadow upon what goes on "down" there and "in" there. The anal inhibitions spread over the genital impulses.

The third source of strength does, I believe, derive from castration anxiety — if we elaborate this into fear of bodily harm. Fantasies of having been castrated (which I have found ubiquitous) give increased, not decreased, validity to the notion that harm can, indeed, come to one. The sexual understanding of the phallic-oedipal period, that the female body is penetrated, arouses acute fear of bodily harm. While castration is always a fantasy, sexual penetration, labor, and childbirth are not. The conviction that she has already been damaged joins with fears arising from wisps of overheard conversation between women, movies of childbirth agonies, the imagined pain of the huge penis; all these give a tenacity to superego power. Sexual arousal itself gives rise to fears that give the superego its power against the sexual arousal. (These fears are quite different from retaliatory fears arising from competition, which are common to both sexes.)

Structure

The resurrected omnipotent mother that lends power to the superego also affects the structure. When a new identification is being made, the earlier ones to which it is related are also resurrected. The new level identification awakens the original relationship upon which it is based. The mother is perceived again through infantile eyes; she is diffuse, unstructured, herself. The ego and superego identifications are with this unclear object whose expectations are unclear. This leads to an internalization of dependence on a superego identification bearing many of the qualities of the resurrected mother (primitive, but often unstable). This quality lends what I would like to call a flexibility to the female superego.

These same early images are resurrected for the boy as well as for the girl. However, during the intervening years of development, there has been a transformation from the mother of early infancy. Through the process of disidentifying from her, through the clear, articulated body images that have helped him in his path toward individuation, through the identifications with the father, the omnipotent mother has been transformed into the omnipotent "father of reality," with whom we are familiar. The diffusiveness and internal orientation have been transformed into external orientation, defined performance (through measurable, defined experiences). The structure of the superego follows these experiences; the images both of the self and of the father with whom superego identifications are made, are clearly articulated; the elements, the prohibitions, and permissions are more clearly defined.

Contents

The last aspect of the superego I will discuss is contents. Many would say that all the issues I have been discussing are the result of superego contents (Applegarth 1976, Blum 1976). The content "be dependent" could explain why women look to others for their values and approval. The content "be my baby, my baby doll" could account for difficulties women report in achieving autonomy. The content "do not think, intellectuality belongs to men" could account for women's complaints of inhibitions in this area. The content "stay at home and take care of your babies" could account for women's difficulty in pursuing careers. The list is endless. (Zilbach et al. 1979 document this well.) This formulation leads to attacks on culture for inhibiting women.

I do not think all can be attributed to content alone; I do not think anything antithetical can long be imposed from without. Without inner sources for these issues, I do not believe they would exist. Women cannot achieve the distance from their origins in the same way that men can, and continue to develop as nurturing mothers. They must remain close to their origins; yet, to achieve autonomy, the most valued attribute in our society (Broverman et al. 1970), they must now disidentify in the same way that men do.

Thinking of the superego in the broader ways I have suggested broadens the range of our therapeutic task. The feminine superego is different in the ways that I have described. The reawakened diffusivity lends flexibility to the structure; the strength has sources earlier, and is related somewhat differently to castration anxiety. The contents carry all the expectations for femininity from the powerful moment of gender assignment. All are created out of developmental experiences within the self and between the self and the outer world. The resurrected mother enters the strength, the structure, and the contents of the female superego, reinforcing, in each aspect, its difference from the male superego.

If control of drives, various manifestations of morality, and characterological conscientiousness are considered indicators of superego development, there is no evidence for the psychoanalytic position that women have defective superegos. Analysts have struggled for decades in attempting to ameliorate powerful primitive superegos in their women patients.

This psychoanalytic position derives from the fact that Freud observed a quality characteristic of men's superegos and used it as a criteria for superego development. The characteristic that he chose was firmness of structure; while this indeed may be different in women than men, it is not an adequate criteria by which to evaluate superego development, but only a single aspect of that development. In this chapter I examine superego development in boys and girls by using three axes: strength, structure, and contents. There could be others.

An additional source of Freud's difficulty in examining women's superegos lies in his chronology for its emergence. In tying superego development to the phallic-oedipal phase, and particularly to castration anxiety, he hypothesized that girls, already "castrated," had no motivation for superego formation. Many analytic observers have noted the early morality and conscientiousness of little girls; most have, like Freud, attributed this to their feelings of having been castrated, perhaps as punishment for masturbation. While there may be a finalizing reorganization of the superego at the end of the oedipal phase, it is my impression that the core of the superego, with its primitive, irrational qualities, is formed much earlier and is revised throughout each stage of development.

In this chapter, I attempt to trace the structure, strength, and contents of the superego to the earliest interaction between the child and the parents and between the child's mental development and its experience of its own body. Both of these experiences, the relationships to the outer and inner world, differ in boys and girls from the moment of birth and form the mental world, both ego and superego.

5

The Female Oedipal Complex

"It is only in the male child that we find the fateful combination of love for the one parent and simultaneous hatred for the other as rival" (Freud 1931, p. 229). Despite this warning, psychoanalytic theory has progressed since its inception using the term *the female Oedipus* as parallel to the Oedipus complex in boys.

The very terms *the oedipal phase* or *the oedipal complex* embody the problem. The Oedipus myth is the story of attempted infanticide, patricide, and consummated incest. It is the story of a son who struggles against his patricidal wishes, against knowledge, at the same time that he commits patricide and ardently pursues knowledge. It is a story of his ultimate fulfillment in power and sexuality, and his horror, guilt, and punishment at what he had indeed accomplished. There is no parallel story for the girl. While conflicts arising out of the pursuit of knowledge exist in girls, the pattern differs; anxieties about knowledge frequently lead to severe inhibitions, both sexual and intellectual. This is a different story from that of Oedipus, who finds fulfillment first and suffers anxieties later. These patterns suggest gender-specific developmental responses to sexual anxieties.

Girls and boys develop differently. Although many of the developmental tasks are the same, the "equipment" they bring to the tasks and the equipment given to them by their parents for solving the tasks vary. These differences have tremendous impact on the solutions to developmental crises and the mastering of developmental challenges. Freud's desire for a unified developmental theory "blinded" him to obvious developmental differences and forced him to cast the female in the mold of the male; this is a very poor fit. Oedipus was a boy.

In this discussion, I will focus on gender-specific issues, anxieties, and modes of mastery.

First, the assignment of gender evokes a wide range of feelings, attitudes, and expectations in both parents, consciously and unconsciously. These early messages are internalized in the mirroring that goes on between mother and child, *and* father and child. They lay the foundation for the girl's negotiating each developmental step; later experiences are assimilated into the earliest ones (see also Tyson 1982).

The second area is in the very anatomy of girls. Freud's statement that anatomy is destiny (1924) focused on only one aspect of anatomy, the penis or lack of it. He considered the childhood of a girl to be characterized by a lack of a genital, her own not to be discovered until adolescence. Here I will try to separate the two issues that the role of anatomy has on girls' development. It seems appropriate to separate the role of the penis and the girl's reaction to it from the role of her own genitals and her reactions to them. The girl's own anatomy is as important in her development as are her reactions to the anatomy of the boy.

Third, the achievement of psychic separation (see Mahler

1968) is enmeshed with issues of gender. Gender sameness and gender difference shape the solution of this developmental task, and the outcome of this phase (separation-individuation) underlies the conflicts aroused by the erotic genital excitement of the Oedipus in several ways that are gender specific.

In contemplating a unique developmental crisis for girls, I wondered whether the Electra myth might be comparable for girls to the Oedipus myth for boys. In discussing this, several scholarly colleagues commented that Freud had originally conceptualized the girl's development as an Electra complex—it seems to be a widely held impression. In Freud, there are three references, each either in parentheses or in a footnote. Each disclaims the relevance of Electra, rejecting the concept as proposed by Jung. (This may have resulted from his conflicts with Jung at this time.) Freud (1931) put it, "We are right in rejecting the term 'Electra Complex' which seeks to emphasize the analogy between the attitude of the two sexes" (p. 229) and (to repeat the opening quote of this chapter, from Freud [1931]) "It is only in the male child that we find the fateful combination of love for the one parent and simultaneous hatred for the other as a rival (p. 229)."

Despite Freud's warning, the female Oedipus has been treated as analogous. There are ways in which girls' experiences are the same as boys and ways in which they differ. Freud pointed to the preoedipal tie to the mother as perhaps more critical to girls' development and to an understanding of that phase of their development, in comparison to the oedipal phase in boys. Current authors (A. Bergman 1982, M. Bergmann 1982, Chasseguet-Smirgel 1970, Oliner 1982, Parens et al. 1976) are addressing some aspects of these issues. Few have attempted to reformulate the oedipal as uniquely feminine. Although Freud dismissed the use of the

Electra myth, it does seem appropriate to review it as potentially prototypical. Many themes that have emerged as prominent in female psychology are rooted in the ancient poetry—themes of frustrated longing, envy, helplessness, revenge, masochism, hatred, and remorse.

Electra is the second daughter of Clytemnestra and Agamemnon, who has been away ten years fighting the Trojan Wars with Menelaus, his brother, in pursuit of Helen, Menelaus's wife and Clytemnestra's sister. Electra's sister, Iphegenia, has been sacrificed by their father in efforts to assuage the gods and win the wars. Her mother has brought into the home her lover, Aegisthus, alluded to as somewhat effeminate, with whom she is ruling in her husband's absence. Electra's brother, Orestes, predecessor to Oedipus, has been sent away from home by Clytemnestra and Aegisthus out of fear that he would not countenance the betrayal of his father implicit in their alliance. Electra, in a rage at her mother for her betrayal of her father with Aegisthus, spends her days waiting for her father to return. When Agamemnon returns and is murdered by his wife, Electra's rage is compounded. She is overwrought and can think only of murderous revenge against her mother. She takes no action, but waits (yet again) for her brother Orestes to murder their mother—manifestly to avenge her father's death. When brother and sister meet, Electra rails against their mother and encourages Orestes to do the deed. Though she is at home and has the opportunity of killing her mother and Aegisthus should she wish (Clytemnestra has already represented the model of a woman as murderess), she does not do so. In Sophocles's version, when she believes that Orestes has died, she begins to take vengeance into her own hands. In the end, Orestes does the slaying while Electra, lamenting, places her hand on her brother's sword.

Clearly, the stories are different. The main theme of the

Oedipus myth used by Freud is that of the triangular love relationship (the rivalry between father and son for the mother), the inevitable longing of every child, the inevitable hatred of every child. More recent authors (Devereux 1953, Ross 1979) have pointed to additional aspects of the story as having universal psychological relevance. The first is the fact that Jocasta and Laius have pierced Oedipus's feet (rendered him impotent) and put him out to die. The second is Oedipus's assumption of all the guilt. Although his parents attempted to murder him, it is Oedipus alone who is overcome with remorse, blinds himself, exiles himself to a tragic death. These terrible wishes, guilt, and punishment are the "stuff" from which our work is made.

Is the "stuff" the same for Electra? Electra does not consummate incest with her father; indeed, she does not even have a sexual life (Electra means "the unmarried"); her life is described as one of "waiting." Electra is not banished or perceived as a danger, as was Orestes (later Oedipus, even later Hamlet). Electra does not murder her mother. Though desiring to, her final participation is feeble and humiliating. Does the Electra myth have any value as a model for a little girl's erotic attachments and conflicts?

Her father is away, her sister has been killed, her brother has been sent away. Electra is left with her mother, who holds sole power to rule. Electra must be angry with her father, although we hear none of that—he is, after all, off with his brother seeking another woman. She cannot help but be enraged at him for leaving her, for murdering her sister. She must have smarted from his indifference to her. To add further insult, her father has many other women, one of whom he brings into the home.

Agamemnon, the prototypical absent father, leaves Electra alone with her mother. A child would surely be angry at her mother for not better protecting her, for not keeping

father at home, for allowing her sister to die and her brother
to be sent away. In the myth, we hear endless accusations of
her mother's unmotherliness. Electra cannot reenter the
protective arms of the maternal embrace. First, mother is
busy with her own sexuality and with making new babies.
Second, disappointment in mother's helplessness and in her
inability to protect her must have revived earlier rages. Thus,
whatever wishes she had herself to be the one in mother's bed
are frustrated.

Enraged at her father for his betrayal of her and her
mother, then enraged at her mother for her betrayal of her
and her father, deprived of her sister and her brother,
Electra presents a picture of lonely helplessness. Comfort
and gratification from either parent are blocked; identifications with either parent are blocked. Electra's plight seems to
describe a position of girls at a critical stage of their
development.

Throughout the plays, there is ongoing hatred and con-
demnation and devaluation of her mother; side by side there
is untarnished idealization of her father, no matter what he
has done. This theme is familiar to us. A boy, blocked in his
gratification, can identify with his father in the positive
Oedipus complex or with his mother in the negative Oedipus
complex. A girl, frustrated in her gratification, is blocked by
developmental issues from making either identification; at
this point she can indeed become a picture of lonely helplessness.

There are several themes that emerge in each of the three
Electras that we may view as being as powerful as the themes
in the Oedipus myth. Some are comparable, some contrast.
Aeschylus presents Electra in two plays, *The Libation
Bearers* and *Eumenides*. Sophocles and Euripides each have
written Electra plays. A look at Electra's pains and passions

may illuminate some specifically female struggles and draw a picture very different from that of Oedipus.

In *The Libation Bearers,* anger, envy, and the first sounding of masochism appear within the triangular situation:

> Pity me;   l. 130
> pity your own Orestes. How shall we be lords
> in our house? We have been sold, and go as wanderers
> because our mother bought herself a man.
> Now I am what a slave is while they go proud
> in the high style and luxury. . . .

And here is the theme of helplessness:

> Meanwhile I   l. 445
> stood apart, dishonored, nothing worth
> in the dark corner, as you would kennel a vicious dog,

Sophocles connects the themes of outrage, envy, masochism, and helplessness:

> What sort of days do you imagine   l. 266
> I spend. . . .
> Watching the ultimate act of insult,   l. 271
> My father's murderer in my father's bed
> With my wretched mother—if mother I should call her,
> this woman that sleeps with him.

as does Euripides:

> —and here is the keynote of my song,   l. 1060
> Mother who bore me, how I wish your mind were healthy.
> Although for beauty you deserve tremendous praise.

> You, long before your daughter came near sacrifice   l. 1069
> the very hour your husband marched away from home,
> were setting your brown curls by the bronze mirror's light.
> Now any woman who works on her beauty when a man
> is gone from home indicts herself as being a whore.

Each addresses Electra's helplessness, her envy of her mother's sexuality, and her rage at her for preferring a man to her children. Electra longs to be her mother's chosen, in place of a man:

> Next. If as you say, our father killed your daughter   l. 1086
> Did I do any harm to you, or did my brother?
> When you killed your husband, why did you not bestow
> the ancestral home on us.

Her vengeance and murderous hatred are rationalized as revenge:

> If murder judges and calls for murder, I will kill   l. 1094
> you—and our own Orestes will kill you—for father.

The themes of jealousy and rage at her mother's sexuality are clear, as are her complaints that mother has not given her, Electra, her proper place, power, and favor, but has abdicated her motherliness in favor of her own interests and pleasure. Father's murder seems an endless source of justification for her relentless judgment of her mother. Clytemnestra defends herself and explains herself, often imploring her daughter to relinquish her endless mourning, mourning that more often seems like a fueling of a rage than a grief or sadness for her loss.

Since this chapter is addressed to the impact of the interaction of parents and children on the child's development, Clytemnestra's voice is important to hear. In attempting to explain her motivations, Clytemnestra pleads, when accused of indecency by Orestes in *The Libation Bearers:*

. . . tell also of your father's vanities. . . .	l. 918
It hurts women to be kept from their men, my child.	l. 920

Sophocles's Clytemnestra is hurt and provoked by Electra:

. . . There is no insolence in myself	l. 524
but being accused by you so constantly	
I give abuse again	
always your father, Nothing else is your pretext—	l. 528

Mother's jealousy of her daughter's love for her father wounds her and she attempts to discredit him. This theme is often sounded in mothers who depreciate their husbands as part of their effort to keep their daughters close:

You would have served the cause of Justice if	l. 528
you had been right-minded.	
For this your father whom you always mourn,	
alone of all the Greeks, had the brutality	
to sacrifice your sister to the Gods, . . .	
This was the act of a father thoughtless	l. 546
or with bad thought. That is how I see it	
even if you differ with me.	

Clytemnestra expresses her ambivalence toward her daughter. On the one hand, "leave me alone!" on the other, she cannot hate her daughter (Sophocles).

Let me live out my life,	l. 650
just as my life is now, to the end uninjured,	
controlling the house of Atreus and the throne	
living with those I love as I do now,	

the good days on our side, and with such children
as do not hate me nor cause me bitter pain.
. . . Mother and child! It is a strange relation.
A mother cannot hate the child she bore
even when injured by it.

In Euripides, mother's bitterness and unbearable sexual
jealousy parallel Electra's feelings toward her:

And dark and lonely were your father's plots against   l. 1011
those he should have loved and least conspired to kill.
. . . If this had been to save the state from siege
     and ruin   l. 1024
if it had helped his home and spared his other children
to rack one girl for many lives, I could have forgiven,
But now for the sake of Helen's lust . . .
I was unfairly wronged in this, yet not for this   l. 1030
would I have gone savage so, nor killed my husband so,
but he came home to me with a mad, god-filled girl
and introduced her to our bed. So there we were,
two brides being stabled in a single stall.

Neither woman can bear being left out of the desired bed. It
stimulates murderous rage; the envy of sexuality is pervasive.
The mother tries to come to terms with her daughter's love
for her father:

My child, from birth you always have adored
     your father.   l. 1102
This is part of life. Some children always love
the male, some turn more closely to their mother than him.
I know you and forgive you. . . . Perhaps I drove
     my hate   l. 1110
too hard against my husband.

Aeschylus's Electra describes herself in words we have all
heard. Electra's rage gives way to an idealization and eroti-

cization of her suffering; she competes with Clytemnestra
for virtue:

> Now I am what a slave is . . .   l. 135
> while they go proud. . . .
> And for myself, grant that I be more temperate   l. 140
> of heart than my mother; that I act with purer hand.

In Sophocles:

> . . . my bed is witness to my all-night sorrowing   l. 94
> dirges for my unhappy father. . . .
> But for my part, I   l. 103
> will never cease my dirges and sorrowful laments.

and toward her brother Orestes, we see the displacement of
the love toward her father:

> I have awaited him always   l. 164
> sadly, unweariedly,
> till I'm past childbearing,
> till I am past marriage
> always to my own ruin.

> I am one wasted in childlessness   l. 186
> with no loving husband for champion.
> . . . I tenant my father's house in the ugly rags   l. 190
> and stand at a scanty table.

Her sexual renunciation and masochism become her
weapon:

> . . . let me tell you, what benefit   l. 352
> I would achieve by giving up my mourning?
> Do I not live? Yes, I know badly, but
> for me enough. And I hurt them.

In Euripides, the choice of suffering is an expression of power, to reverse the hurt and shame:

I am not forced, I chose this slavery myself   l. 57
. . . and cry my pain to Father in the great bright air.   l. 59
For my own mother, she . . .
has thrown me out like dirt from the house, to her
    husband's joy   l. 61
and while she breeds new children in Aegisthus' bed
has made me and Orestes aliens to her love.

Suffering itself becomes a source of erotic pleasure:

Come, waken the mourning again   l. 125
bring me the sweetness of tears.

. . . while I lift music of mourning   l. 141
by night to my father . . .
as I move ripping my flesh with sharp   l. 147
nails, fists pounding my clipped
head for your dying.
Ai, ai, tear my face!
. . . who calls to its parent so dearly loved   l. 153
. . . And I! I in a peasant's hut   l. 207
waste my life like wax in the sun,
thrust and barred from my father's home
to a scarred mountain exile
while my mother rolls in her bloody bed
and plays at love with a stranger.

Electra's own sexual anxieties are spelled out in Euripides. Talking to a disguised Orestes, who does not threaten her manifestly, she says:

Get out; don't touch. You have no right to touch
    my body.   l. 223

When asked to describe herself to her absent brother, her first words are:

> . . . First, my body, wasted and dry —   l. 239
> Next, my head razor-cropped like a victim of
>   the Scythians.   l. 241

Of her husband:

> He has never been violent or touched me in my bed.   l. 255

Bitterly, speaking of her mother, the longing for both the maternal and sexual are combined:

> Women save all their love for lovers, not for children.   l. 265

Throughout the plays, there is not a single piece of dialogue between Electra and her father Agamemnon, or between her and her stepfather Aegisthus. Greek drama made such plentiful use of conversations with the spirits of the dead, of narrating past conversation, of fantasizing future ones, that I consider this a significant omission. Nor does the Chorus, carrier of much history, description, nuance, and emotion, elaborate the passionate force in Electra. Electra addresses her father's grave (Aeschylus). Here one can hear the echo of the little girl's wish to be the wife as, bringing prayers, she says:

> Shall I say I bring it to the man   l. 89
> beloved, from a loving wife, and mean my mother?

The Chorus, like Clytemnestra, accuses the girl of excessive idealization of her father:

> In reverence for your father's tomb as if it were   l. 106
> an altar,

In Sophocles, the daughter spends her nights in grief:

> And again in the house of my misery   l. 92
> my bed is witness to my all-night sorrowing. . . .
>
> I will not   l. 132
> leave my mourning for my poor father.

The Chorus reflects mother's accusations, and urges Electra to relinquish her stance:

> You have won for yourself   l. 216
> superfluity of misfortune,
> breeding wars in your sullen soul
> evermore.

The daughter is determined to hold onto her love and suffering:

> These ills of mine shall be called cureless   l. 230
> and never shall I give over my sorrow.

Not only does she hold on, she enjoys spitefully and exhibitionistically making them suffer:

> No, this I will not —   l. 818
> live with them anymore. Here, at the gate
> I will abandon myself to waste away
> this life of mine, unloved.

In Euripides, she settles for being a princess of suffering instead of the princess of her great father:

> . . . would my filthy locks   l. 184
> and robe all torn into slavish rags
> do public honor to Agamemnon's

daughter, the princess?
Honor to Troy which will never forget
my conquering father?

The daughter needs father to control mother. She is helpless
to master her envy and rage without him:

"There goes the queen's husband." It was never "the king's
     wife."   l. 931
O, what perversion, when the woman in the house
stands out as master, not the man. I shake in hate
to see those children whom the city knows and names
not by their father's name but only by their mother's.

Her love for her mother appears only after the murder, her
first insightful reflection:

Weep greatly for me, my brother, I am guilty.   l. 1182
A girl flaming in hurt I marched against
the mother who bore me.

What in the Electra myth is comparable to Oedipus?
Clearly, they are different stories. Is Electra's relation to her
father merely a pretext, as Clytemnestra claims, for Electra's
"constant clamor" against her mother, or does this preoccupation with her absent father represent an important position for girls at a time in their development comparable to
the boy's oedipal phase?

Oedipus finds fulfillment after the murder of his father.
He takes over his father's palace. He achieves sexual fulfillment in Jocasta's bed; he rules from his father's throne.
Gradually, anxiety, remorse, self-flagellation, and guilt
emerge and inhibit infinite gratification. For Electra, the tale
is very different. The murder of Clytemnestra does not win
her anything but the beginning of remorse. There is no
sexual fulfillment with her father (or stepfather). Indeed,

there is no sexual fulfillment with anyone. Over and over again, in all three plays, we hear sounded the themes of sexual renunciation and self-flagellation. Her mourning and tears have taken on a "sweetness" of their own as she "lies in bed each night." The mourning seems itself to have become a source of great pleasure. This theme, the erotization of suffering and pain, is familiar as a characteristic often found in female psychology and considered by Freud (1931) and Deutsch (1944) to be a part of normal female development.

Outstanding in all three tales is the idealization of Agamemnon, her father. His actual behavior merits little admiration — he deserted his family, murdered his daughter, was a known womanizer. Where is the girl's hurt, outrage, rage toward such an unrewarding, neglectful, unloving, unprotecting father? There is not a trace in any of the three plays of a basis for this idolizing love — no hint of devotion, play, attention, or interest.

She dismisses Clytemnestra's reminders of her father's behavior. She disregards *his* absence, which really leaves mother in total control, his promiscuous sexuality, his willingness to sacrifice his daughter to his own end. She maintains an idealized image of a pure, noble warrior, fighting for honor. This absent idealized father would be a proper king and rule mother properly and, most important, restore Electra to her proper place as princess. The princess image, so common in mythology, fairy tales, and everyday life, contains several components important to girls' development. It contains an affectionate, admiring, but desexualized relationship with her father, and it confers status on the daughter within the family. It bestows a certain amount of authority and power in the household, granted her by her participation in the king's power. The princess is the opposite of Cinderella.

It is my impression that the Electra myth describes a point

in female development when the girl must integrate her sexuality into her self-image, achieving a childhood identity synthesis. This must contain a stable, individuated self-image with sexuality integrated into her core-gender identity. In order to achieve this, satisfying relationships and identifications with *both* parents are critical.

Electra, frustrated in her erotic longings and in her need for her father, both to confirm her femininity and as a figure of identification, cannot achieve satisfactory resolution. Agamemnon's total disregard for her leaves her alone with both erotic and preerotic ties to her mother. She does not regress to becoming her mother's baby, nor does she relinquish her rage at her mother or her longing for both parents. She cannot go forward and cannot go back. She is a picture of lonely helplessness with her rage and sexuality merged into masochism.

This picture is dramatically different from that of Oedipus. Oedipus is not helpless but kills his confronter and provoker, Laius, and takes his place. This could be seen as constituting an identification with the aggressor, and is usually considered an appropriate identification. Resolution is more complex for girls because such an identification with the early mother, without intervening identifications with her father, would resurrect threatening, reengulfing regression. Whereas Oedipus can take his fate into his own hands, Electra must depend on others to rescue her. The boy could be seen as achieving mastery more narcissistically (through the use of his weapon); the girl's efforts at mastery are more object embedded.

As I turn from the moving portrait painted by the ancient poets, the return to the ordinary language of psychoanalytic discourse seems prosaic. I will attempt to spell out the themes in the poetry that seem to illustrate gender-specific issues.

GENDER-SPECIFIC CONFLICTS
DURING THE OEDIPAL PHASE

Freud viewed the girl at this time in her life as turning toward her father out of disappointment and rage at her mother. The disappointment resulted from the girl's discovery that mother did not *have* a penis; the rage, from the fact that mother did not *give her* a penis. The "turn" was not to father, the person, but to father, the possessor of the desired penis. Parens and colleagues (1976) properly question the formulations in which boys are propelled into a phase of development by unfolding biology, and girls by a narcissistic injury.

Freud saw as one of the burdening tasks for girls at this time a "change of object," from mother to father; the little boy, on the other hand, does not have to negotiate this, but can continue directing his erotic feeling at his original object, his mother. Further burdening the girl's development was relinquishing the longed for penis without hope of knowledge of her own genitals, considered to be inert for many years to come. In essence, she would have to relinquish sexuality altogether. Horney (1924) challenged this notion, asserting that an "undiscovered" genital was a repressed one — by the girl and, clearly, by Freud himself.

It is startling to find in Nagera, as late as 1975, "from the ego point of view, we have to take into account that this phallic Oedipal stage is usually accompanied by the belief that all human beings possess a phallus, including, of course, the mother" (p. 120). From an ego point of view, this belief would make female children severely defective in reality testing. The wish to have a penis, the fantasy of having lost or maybe growing one inside, is a very different matter (one I shall take up more fully later as penis envy).

For boys, this phase may well be dominated by destructive

impulses toward the father in order to seize and hold onto mother for himself. I believe that the preoedipal longings for a mother from whom he is separated by both anatomy and society fuel the erotic oedipal fires (as indeed, in the tale of Oedipus, whose mother, Jocasta, sent him away when he was an infant).

The story seems different for girls. There is not the preponderance of destructive, hostile fantasies to anywhere near the extent that they appear in boys. This difference is clearly manifest in children's play and choice of toys, usually by the time they are 3 (Galenson and Roiphe 1976, Kestenberg 1956a). What has emerged clinically, over the years, is frighteningly intense envy (as in both Electra and Clytemnestra) and an equally frightening, equally intense wish to be envied. While the character trait of envy appears in men as well as women, it has long been considered a feminine trait. It is often interpreted as penis envy; Grossman and Stewart (1976) have focused on earlier roots of envy but have not differentiated why this might be a more common character trait in women. Women express their wishes to be the best dressed, or to have the best husband, to be the most beautiful, sexual one. The accompanying fantasy is that other women will stand and look on, filled with admiration and envy, and feel themselves lessened and humiliated. "When I am big and you are little . . ." is such a common phrase for the little girl. Whether motivated by a power struggle, by sexual competitiveness, or by narcissistic injury, the dominant fantasy seems to be a reversal of childhood humiliations. In order to attain this, one crucial element differentiates these women's fantasies from men's. That is, in order to be envied, the object must be maintained, not destroyed. Electra's envy of her mother is manifestly clear; she envies the person who is in her bed, in her house, and who has her mother's love; she lives in humiliation. Envy is a connecting intense feeling toward another person, an expression of involvement.

The formulation "change of object" is disconcerting. It is parallel to the phrase "turn to the father," used in connection with separation-individuation. In 1966, Forest proposed renaming the oedipal phase the "family triangle." In that paper, she reminds us that the child is born to two parents, not just to his or her mother. Unique relationships develop between the child and each of the parents. Considerable recent research has demonstrated that fathers and mothers relate differently to boy and girl children from birth on. The "father of separation" (Mahler 1974) has had an earlier history. That he exists clearly is demonstrated in a study by Brooks and Lewis (1975), reported by Formanek (1982), in which 25 percent of 15-month-old infants named pictures of their fathers correctly, and no infant named the mother correctly.

What occurs at the phase of childhood genital preoccupation is an integration of erotic feeling into the preexisting relationship with the father. The erotic longings toward him and the frustration of those longings are assimilated; the success or failure of this developmental crisis is dependent on the earlier relationships.

In contrast to the trends in American psychoanalysis that perceive a mother–child unit with the father as an outsider disrupting the sublime bond is the approach to the first year of life taken by Melanie Klein (1975) and by those who have used her theories as the basis for their own thinking. The contrast is startling. Here we have the infant intuitively perceiving in the earliest months of life that there is an other – the father; that he is a competitor for the mother; that he has a penis that the child wants to steal for himself and use to fill up the mother; and that the child wishes to attack babies in the mother's stomach. The oedipal in an archaic form is present in the same first year of life seen as so sublime by others.

Four women in analysis gave birth during the course of our work; all the babies were born within three months. For three, the baby was a first child; for the fourth, it was the second child, but the first in a new marriage. All talked extensively about the impact of the child on their relationships with their husbands; all felt a terrible disruption and loss of the exclusivity; all were terribly jealous (although also delighted) of the husband's attention to the babies, and three of the women experienced a clear revival of their wishes to be daddy's favorite as their husbands became daddies. All reported similar reactions in their husbands. They wanted exclusivity; preference emerged in otherwise not usually jealous relationships. Yet another feature clear in all was each mother's intense desire to be the one person the baby wanted most, almost exclusively. Even though several of these women were professionals who wished for their husbands' active participation, when they saw the fathers with their babies, all experienced considerable jealousy.

A new mother, a patient who had a long struggle to marry and have a child, said, "It's so funny, I kiss my little girl all over her body. You know, I don't think I would feel as free to do that with a little boy. I think I would be inhibited." Hence, the sexual potential of the male infant as a source of influence on the erotic spontaneous behavior of a young mother toward her infant demonstrates the impact of gender on two things simultaneously. First, there is the impact on the mother, who feels the sexual implications of kissing her boy baby all over. Second, the girl baby is "kissed all over," that is to say, her body is accessible for erotization and she experiences more general, frequent erotization. Numerous studies (Barglow and Schaefer 1976) have demonstrated that little girls are held more frequently, for longer periods, by their mothers. Various authors have stressed different facets of this behavior. Little girls remain closer to their mothers in play and stranger situations. Explanations range; Barglow and Schaefer emphasize the girl's smaller size, the ease with which she can be comforted. Contrasted to the boy, the girl remains in an undisturbed, narcissistic, symbiotic relationship to the mother for a longer time. The young mother's freedom to kiss her daughter's body freely suggests that further contributions may come from the larger measure of nonconflictual erotization of the girl.

Further, the mother's perception of the girl as part of herself increases the symbiotic tie—we are one. Another young mother reported, "My baby doesn't look at me all the time now. I used to look at her especially when nursing and say to myself, 'That's me.' Now she moves away, looks around. She isn't me anymore." The confluence of material from infant observation, from mothers' own reports, and from women in analysis seems to point to an intense relationship with the mother, with the symbiotic, undifferentiated aspects of that relationship more pronounced and prolonged than in boys.

To return to the young mother who felt so different in the kissing of her baby girl and reflected that this might be inhibited with a boy, it seems to me that in both positions (the idealization of the mother–child dyad and the Kleinian sexualization of the infantile period) there is a considerable degree of projection of the infantile fantasies and idealizations of the theorizer. It is more likely that awareness of the infant's potential for sexual gratification resides in the parent viewing, holding, caressing the child, than in the infant. That something of this becomes integrated into the total relationship between parents and their opposite sex children is surely true and desirable. To the extent that the child internalizes the parents' views of it, he or she feels desired as well as desirable. Feeling desirable, touchable, kissable then contributes to the unfolding of the gender-specific identification and plays a large role in the infant's becoming masculine or feminine and in the later erotic-dominated phase and even later in adult self-image consolidation.

To the extent that the parents perceive the child as (unconsciously, usually) potentially sexual, to that extent all of their conflicts about their own sexuality are rearoused, and their comfort or discomfort with both same-sex and opposite-sex bodies enters into the relationship with their babies. The parents' fantasies will affect the fantasies the child forms as he or she moves through the developmental stages. During the same week in which the mother reported her great comfort in kissing her girl baby, another mother of a baby almost the same age reported how much she loved kissing her new son's little body—his belly, his feet. The sexual component emerged in the associations, which led her to comment on the impact of the baby on her and her husband's life-style. The associations moved on to their own nudity and what impact this might have on the baby, who just loves to look at everything, and to their sexual life, in which she tends to be noisy. What must that sound like to a baby? A dream the night following that session led to her own shameful memory of mutual examination of the genitals with a little girlfriend when she was 7. Clearly, the personal combinations of conflicts aroused are infinite, but every parent will experience them in relation to the sexuality of his or her child.

The intensity of the meaning of becoming parents, the revival of the rivalrous feelings from their own childhoods, shape the mood, handling, and communications to the child about him- or herself and their attitudes toward him or her. The child who is a threatening rival to his or her mother or father soon picks up some of the danger of this position, and these very early attitudes, these preverbal communications, will have their impact later, when sexual rivalry is the central issue.

GENITAL ANXIETIES
DURING THE OEDIPAL PHASE

I will now discuss briefly what I have defined elsewhere as specific female genital anxieties. (For a fuller discussion, see Chapter 3.) They are differentiated from what are usually referred to as genital anxieties — castration anxiety and penis envy.

There has been an indiscriminate use of the term "castration anxiety." It is generally used to refer to a host of fears and fantasies about lost, damaged, or missing parts of the body. While these fears appear during girls' development, and in women's analyses, it is incorrect to describe these female fears exclusively in the language and imagery of boys' and men's anxieties. If one does not too precipitously name the anxiety being expressed but investigates more closely, one finds a host of fears of different descriptions. Many are predominantly female anxieties, although they may appear in men as well. Unfortunately, as in discussing the Oedipus complex, there is no single tidy word to describe these fears in the female.

The term *access* seems to describe several of the girl's anxieties. By access I mean several different issues. The girl does not have ready access to her genital; this touches on many levels of experience. First, she cannot see it as she and the boy can see the boy's genitals. This creates immense difficulty in forming a mental representation of her body, in which there are intense physical sensations.

Second, she cannot touch and manipulate it in a desexualized way, therein gathering tactile, visual, and sensual knowledge of her body that is not forbidden or tied to forbidden fantasies. There is no mastery of this part of her body.

Third, and very central, it is a body opening over which there is no control, no opening or closing, as there is with the mouth and anus; girls feel they cannot control access by others or by themselves. Sexual arousal occurs seemingly spontaneously, without the girl's active part in generating it. It is frightening to have an open hole; things can come out and go in, there is no way to close or open it, no control over access.

Related, and becoming prominent at the time of heightened erotic interest, is the awareness that access can put her in danger. Girls have "penetration" anxiety. Not only can things go in and out, but things that can potentially harm her. Girls fear damage to their little bodies from the exciting paternal penis. And, very early, they fear the damage to their bodies from the longing for babies they want to create. In addition to these experiences that are specific to the open, or access issues, there are others.

Sexual arousal stimulates multiple body sensations, both internal and external. The excitement is diffuse and cannot be defined as a specific physical sensation or in language (Montgrain 1983); this excitement generates ego diffusion as well as physical diffusion—a state most desired and most feared. The more intense the sensuality, the more it threatens engulfment (Montgrain 1983). Like physical pain, it can feel like an attack from within (Klein 1945, McDougal 1984).

This variety of specific female anxieties focuses on access, control, and diffusivity and leads to specific developmental efforts at mastery that are typical of female development. In reporting children's reactions to sexual differences, Galenson and Roiphe (1976) noted differences in the reactions of boys

and girls. Boys became mildly hyperactive, chose toys considered typically masculine, and masturbated fairly vigor-
ously from then on. They reported that the girls in their
study demonstrated anal and urethral confusion, oral-
regressive behavior, and anal zone exploration and masturbation. They describe this as "castration anxiety." I view this
behavior as a turn to prior modes of mastery—manipulation, opening and closing, holding in and expelling. Being in
control is possible in these body areas in ways that the girl's
own genital does not offer. I would describe the boys'
hypercathexis of the penis, their increased masturbation, and
increased focus on male toys as *evidence* of castration
anxiety, with their mode of mastery (defense) as counterphobic. I would describe the girls' reaction as *genital* anxiety and
their turn (regression) to zones in which they had established
mastery, their pattern of defense. In discussing similar
issues, Parens and colleagues (1976) describe a little girl who
demonstrated the regressions reported by Galenson and
Roiphe; again, they call this a castration reaction. They also
report a turn to the mother and others as an aid in regaining
body control. This dependence on others for gaining body
control differs from boys, for whom their own activity and
familiarity with their genital, and its ready access, permit
more independence from others in pursuit of mastery of the
anxiety.

PENIS ENVY FROM A "DIFFERENTIATION PERSPECTIVE"

Freud's concept, that a girl's wish for a penis leads her to
take her father—as the possessor of the penis—as a libidinal
object, does not address the level of object relations implied
in this formulation, namely, that all objects are defined in

terms of gratification only. Barnett (1968) discusses the penis as a "part object"; she reflects that the boy has the part object with which to satisfy mother, but the girl does not. Part, then, of penis envy in girls could be traced to the knowledge that she is not an acceptable (or sufficient) sexual partner for her mother. This was expressed most dramatically in a session with a lesbian woman who was suffering inconsolable, enraging pain when her partner left her for a man. Her words were, "Why, why, wasn't I enough?"

Fathers have long been viewed as needed to confirm for little girls their femininity, including their sexual desirability. In the father–daughter relationship in which a father cannot do this, his little daughter may feel she does not have the equipment to attract him—that is, a penis. In these terms, penis envy may reflect the feeling of not having the proper equipment to attract either parent, neither mother nor father. And this is, after all, a position that every girl child finds herself in.

Certainly Freud's classic formulation (1925) applies. A little clitoris compares unfavorably with a big (paternal) penis, but also with a little penis. A colleague recently reported a young patient as saying she has such a little spot for pleasure compared to "all" that men have. We can assume from this that this is a woman who has repressed her internal sexual experience (Horney 1924).

The wish for a boundary can be expressed as penis envy. A boundary can have many functions. A boundary can mediate access, in and out. A boundary can define. Montgrain (1983) feels there is a general underestimation of the "overflowing capacity of women's sexuality" (p. 169) that "escapes" the link of language. "There is an insufficient anchorage in anatomical reality" that has a "correlative effect at the symbolic level" (p. 170). This concurs with my own hypothesis (Chapter 3) that sensuality recreates diffusivity from which girls are trying to escape. Montgrain suggests that the wish for a penis contains a wish for the visible, concrete organ that could mobilize castration anxiety and the ensuing controls.

The wish for a penis may reflect a longing for an aid in differentiation. Women's and girls' endless struggles with their mothers reveal an unending struggle for differentiation, complicated for them not only by the normal developmental battles, but by the underlying and unbroken primary identification that is rooted in the undifferentiated state of development.

The central conflict for girls seems to me to be individuation, not castration. The sense of oneness with mother must be maintained for female gender identity to flower into an individuated feminine self; the sense of oneness must be disrupted for the girl to develop an individuated femininity or womanhood. This contradiction underlies and affects developmental conflicts pervasively for girls. While it is clear that early union with mother is critical for boys' development and affects their personality, it is nowhere near as central an issue for them. Union with mother implies a blurring or a noncreation of boundaries between the child's emerging psyche and that of the mother. This is manifest in poor self-image so characteristic of our female patients. Self remains poorly defined and constantly in danger of being affected by the emotional attitudes and expectations of those other people in our patient's world. Others seem to retain for women attributes comparable to the infant girl's experience with the mother, in which the girl both participates in the mother's identity and sees herself reflected in the mother's perception of her and expectations for her.

Freud notes some of these qualities in women — a dependency upon men, an ongoing need for admiration — but he interprets them as evidence of an unresolved oedipal longing.

He did not see these qualities as reflecting a central female developmental issue. To reinterpret, defining the self through the view of the other, of whom one is a part, describes a less sharply defined self and a repetition on the genital level of an earlier pattern. In the four cases of new mothers that I referred to earlier, each was troubled by renewed fears of being one with mother, becoming mother, getting lost in the swamp of mother. These anxieties emerged parallel with delights and joys in becoming "mother," competitive wishes and anxieties about replacing or outdoing mother. Three, in the struggle against the regressive pull and anxiety about losing themselves, clutched onto their professional work. (The fourth was depressed throughout the first six months.) All described their heads as clearing when they were at work. All described a clear, potent feeling; and dreams and associations clearly defined these feelings of effectiveness as having underlying fantasies of being like father, or having a penis. The analytic task became one of integrating competence with femininity.

This gives rise to the most feared image of all — that of the competent, omnipotent mother of infancy. With that omnipotent mother image is aroused the girl's own grandiosity, an aspect of union with mother that has received far too little attention.

Grandiosity is a very powerful factor in women's unconscious, and anxiety and guilt over this residue of infancy are defended against mightily by the resurrection of the helplessness that is the other side of infantile grandiosity. It is one of those areas in which culture contributes by supporting one aspect of the inherent conflict. The secret feeling that she could do anything if permitted is not an uncommon fantasy in women, but it is frequently unconsciously anxiety provoking. Infantile grandiosity, expressed in "I can do anything," is, on the other hand, encouraged in boys, and it leads them to another set of difficulties, in that reality rarely matches the infantile expectations, and they often find themselves wanting. This is not infrequently expressed in phallic terms but does, I believe, have its origins in the infantile "union with mother" phase of development.

Fast's formulation (1979), that the wish to retain infantile omnipotence is a defense against gender differentiation and integration, is relevant here. I have seen the expression of total grandiosity most clearly expressed in an egocentric way in pregnant women. During pregnancy, the female attains heights of omnipotence rarely accorded the male. The omnipotent creator experiences the unconscious fantasies from every phase. She embodies the phallus, both through what it has given to her, and through its unconscious identity with anal body contents. The grandiosity of the anal phase and the exultation at having valued body contents merge with a fantasy of being truly the omnipotent mother (and baby) of infancy.

The mother's grandiosity and omnipotence are not only admired but terribly feared, and hence need to be denied. Mother is hated and must be deflated by children of both sexes. For the girl, because she is a participant in the mother's identity, the hatred and deflation directed against the mother are automatically directed against the self, contributing to female masochism. There are residues and derivatives of infantile grandiosity that women also defend against. Many are well aware, in their relations with men toward whom they are overtly and consciously subservient and toward whom they have a humble attitude, that they have within them the power to make the male, particularly the sexual partner, feel extremely inadequate and inept. By just a flicker of an expression, a woman can say, "You are nothing, I am everything." It is often expressed in sexual relationships by a woman's attitude, "It is your job to satisfy me." It was perfectly expressed to me by a neighbor who encountered a young exhibitionist in the lobby of her building. Upon her entering, he opened his raincoat, awaiting her fear and fright as he exhibited his power to her. She, having had five brothers, looked at him and said, "I've seen bigger and better, I have five brothers." And with that, the young exhibitionist's erection dropped. These words can wither practically any man, and each man is vulnerable from the time that he himself envied all those who were bigger and better. The knowledge that she has such power is frightening to the woman, in that she must rely on males for a number of psychic necessities developmentally. The idealization of the male and his penis is essential to her; hence, an exaggeration of helplessness is mobilized in her and culturally supported as a defense. The reconnecting in a female with her participation in the mother's grandiosity is an important element in the analyses of women, as competence cannot be integrated so long as it feels antagonistic to her femininity.

FATHER AND DAUGHTER

The analytic literature on the father–daughter relationship is astonishingly sparse. (The *Chicago Index of Psychoanalytic Literature* contained no such topic until 1983, although there were pages of articles on the father–son or father–child relationship.) Considering that Freud's earliest cases and theories were built upon female patients who experienced him as father, and that, over the years, most analyses have been of women with male analysts, this deficit is even more dramatic. Here I will attempt to synthesize some of the findings reported by child observers, data from research, and data from child, adolescent, and adult analyses.

Freud did not contemplate a significant relationship between the father and daughter until the oedipal phase. Even at this late stage in development, the father's role seems insignificant, in that he is only sought out as the possessor of the penis the girl supposedly so ardently desires (out of envy to possess, not as a source of sexual pleasure). Preoedipal and pregenital seem relegated to a misty period in which all that is clear of the father is his penis, its representation as breast or feces, and its role in the relationship to the mother, the only true libidinal object.

Studies in direct child observation, the expansion of our understanding of the libidinal phases to include many aspects of psychic development that proceed simultaneously with the movement from libidinal stage to stage, have demystified some of preoedipal, pregenital development. This requires a rethinking of the role of the father in the girl's psychic development.

Increasing attention has been given to the father's role in development, although the predominant focus has, for decades, been the mother–child interaction, almost to the exclusion of the father. Mahler has focused on the father as rescuer from the symbiotic tie to mother, coming toward the child "from outer space," as a "knight in shining armor" (Mahler, cited by Abelin 1971, p. 232). More recent observers report different findings. Abelin, who studied these early ties to the father intensely, reports that Schaffer and Emerson (Abelin 1971, p. 232) found that infants who formed strong attachments to their mothers formed strong attachments to their fathers as well, a few weeks or months later; all children studied formed strong attachments to both parents by 18 months.

Ilg and Ames (1955) report that the infant "particularly likes his father's low voice" (p. 17) at 28 weeks. Abelin (1971, p. 234) cites a study by Mohaczy in which a mild stranger reaction to the father only appeared among infants whose fathers did not interact frequently with them. Abelin himself (1971) found precursors of attachment to fathers very early, lagging slightly behind such reactions to mother and siblings; all but one of the infants observed showed recognition of their fathers by a happy smile before age 6 months, and were strongly attached to their fathers by 9 months. He found that the amount of father–infant interaction influenced the timing and intensity of the attachment. Stranger reactions to the fathers were very rare, occurring only before 6 months and even then only in states of severe distress or if the father had been absent. Many were observed to "prefer" the father; one girl was reported to have always preferred him. In two cases where the preference for the father was clear, there was a noted disturbance in the infant–mother cueing.

When the child moves from infancy into the toddler phase, the relationship with the father becomes markedly different from that to the mother; the father is more attuned to the "wild exuberance" (Abelin 1971, p. 239), while the mother is turned to more for comfort at times of distress or fatigue. The girls in Abelin's study attached themselves earlier and more intensely to their fathers than the boys. They were nonetheless wary of other men. Girls "maintained closer and more specific ties to both parents and were more guarded toward strangers than were the boys" (p. 242). As the toddler moved into the rapprochement subphase, the mother was more ambivalently cathected, while the father continued to be experienced as a "stable island" (p. 243). Fathers were not found to be objects of rivalry at a time when other children were clear rivals, until the end of the third year. A few weeks after the rapprochement crisis, father images were evoked in play, stories, and picture books when toddlers became disappointed with their mothers; this suggests that a stable, usable internalized image of father has been achieved. Abelin suggests that the task of intrapsychic separation between mother and child "might be *impossible for either of them to master without their having the father to turn to*" (p. 248). This need long predates the arrival of the oedipal father.

Kleeman (1976) stresses the impact of gender identity and the development of cognitive functions in his discussion of the girl's early development. From the moment of gender assignment, a process begins in the interaction between the parents and girl that becomes the data from which she constructs a self-image. The developing cognitive functions permit the development of categorization (into male and female); this is conveyed through parents and identification mechanisms. Labeling herself is, in Kleeman's view, absolutely primary. Even identification processes, so central in the analytic understanding of gender identity, would be guided by the labeling. Not only will her own gender become organized according to labeling, but the opposite gender as well.

The discovery of anatomical differences usually follows at least a year's experience with both parents and differentiated relationships with each, including different responses to her from each parent. It is into this already evolving organization that the anatomical differences are assimilated. Hence, one might see the increase in activity reported by Galenson and Roiphe (1976) not as simply a hypercathexis of his penis (as discussed earlier in this chapter), but also as a mobilization of the kinds of responses selectively encouraged by both parents during the preceding years of life, that is, encouraging activity and the handling of the penis. The girl's return to her mother and other regressive movements not only reflect the inner-genital confusion, but also repeat the patterns of behavior and comfort encouraged by the mother in earlier experiences. I have already noted (Chapter 4) that part of the gender assignment of which Kleeman speaks includes the mother's earliest expectation of the boy's difference from her and the girl's sameness; this orients the mother to encourage the boy to move away from her and the girl to continue to turn toward her.

THE OEDIPAL DANGERS

The prime danger to the boy during this exciting time seems to be the threat of castration, and the conflicts he experiences are an outgrowth of the fear of damage to his already overvalued penis (in that it can be carrying for him the burden of separation).

As in the boy, the girl's body integrity is threatened. For the girl, the body danger comes from the fantasy of having gratification; for the boy, the danger comes as punishment for the gratification. Like Oedipus, he can have his fun but he must pay with fear that he will be punished. Although fear of danger to the penis from the woman's genitals is not uncommon, it is the fear of punishment that has always seemed most prominent in male psychology. For the girl, however, genital excitement arouses anxiety over control and opening, and the fantasy of penetration itself gives rise to fantasies of invasion, tearing, and damaging. Side by side with the danger of sexual fulfillment is the danger of pregnancy and childbirth. The baby stimulates fantasies of being overstuffed, of having her insides pushed around. The fear of sex and childbirth is known early to little girls, or fantasized from "woman talk" and recently more graphically from television. When little boys talk about sex, it is with excitement and anticipation; for girls this same excitement is contaminated with danger.

PARENTAL RELATIONSHIPS AND
IDENTIFICATION

Aside from the body fear, the relationships with both parents present inherent problems that impede the resolution of the childhood genital crisis. Father, who has been a rescuer from the relationship with mother, the "first other," the "knight in shining armor," the "representative of reality," the "stable island," "uncontaminated by ambivalence," becomes dangerous as well as exciting at this time. The father seems to have *been* a haven, now disrupted by the intense genital elements introduced into the relationship.

In addition to the dangers now present in the father–daughter relationship, new dangers are introduced into the already troublesome mother–daughter relationship. The conflicts and possible resolutions in this position are different for girls as Freud (1925) long ago noted.

While the girl had to rely more on the emotional support, presence, and identifications with her parents during earlier phases and crises in development, the very fiber of her feminine identity is under siege during this phase due to the intense conflicts in entering the identifications with both parents. In order to integrate sexuality into her femininity, clearly the girl must effect an adequate identification with her mother. Since no new identification is built (Reich 1954), the old identifications along with the intense conflicts and pleasure saturating them are reawakened, and these both impede and promote the genital identifications. The threat of merger implied in being one with mother produces anxiety; being different from her disrupts the very oneness with her that must be at the core of femininity.

Perhaps the girl's early connection with her father that is reported by Abelin (1971) could be understood as a very early differentiating experience — his parenting style, his way of relating to her. M. Bergmann (1982), commenting on the move from dyad to triad, felt puzzled about what generates this movement. It may be that the movement is motivated by the presence and importance of the "other" from the very beginning. Father's very way of relating to his daughter differs from mother's. As clearly as the mother experiences her daughter as like herself, so does the father, clearly, distinctly, sometimes overtly, experience his daughter as different from himself. His expectations, perceptions, and treatment of her all enhance her developing sense of a self separate from the mother. Abelin assumes that some of the relationship with the father is colored by and emerges from the symbiotic phase, suggesting that some integration of the self-experience would include early bodily experiences fused with father.

Some girls tend to see father as more nurturant than boys do. Whether this reflects a safe transfer of nurturance to an object who does not threaten reengulfment, or the nature of the father's handling of the little girl, we cannot determine. The derivatives are clear enough in the girl's and woman's turn to father/husband for support and comfort, often to the exclusion of their mothers.

While the father's task of aiding the boy in disidentifying with the mother has long been recognized, the same task is necessary for girls to achieve individuation. However, as in so many aspects of their development, it is a more complex task. The mutual same-sex body facilitates the identification between father and son. There is the inherent problem for both father and daughter in identifying with someone so physically different. For the girl, it is disruptive of the generational mother–daughter tie that must be maintained for femininity to flourish. In addition, many men find it impossible to allow, let alone promote, their daughters' identification with them (see Leonard 1966). In their own efforts to differentiate, to establish and maintain maleness, boys use a number of defensive maneuvers that can interfere when they become fathers rearing daughters. The boy who uses his maleness toward women to maintain superiority over the seemingly omnipotent mother of childhood may well be unable to allow his daughter to be like him. Torok (1970) would refer to this position as: he can thank women for being castrated; the anatomical difference secures him against reengulfment. This stance, reflected in men's activities, schools, and clubs, has had a prominent place as a culturally supported defense against the threat of engulfment or loss of disidentification from mother. To the extent that his narcissistic integrity as a man relies on such a structure, such a father could not encourage his daughter's identification with him, so necessary for girls to establish their own autonomy.

That paternal interest and availability seem vital for development of autonomy-derived activities of initiative and independence has been demonstrated in a number of studies. Lynn (1974) reports on research indicating that better functioning, more independent daughters who did well in school and reported higher self-esteem had fathers who showed active interest in their activities. Fathers who treated daughters with more warmth and less interest had more dependent, less successful daughters. Studies of the effects of father absence on quantitative skills reveal that girls with absent fathers did poorly; the more absent the father, the poorer the performance.

Gray (1959), Helper (1955), and Osgood and colleagues (1957) report that girls perceived as being like their fathers are more admired than those perceived as being like their mothers. What an impossible position! The girl's need to be like father has been discussed thoroughly by Harley (1971), who sees prepubescent girls as reworking earlier developmental issues in preparation for puberty. Her focus is on the issue of genital confusion in penis envy. She comments that girls who play with boys feel stronger, much as Forest (1966) and Glover and Mendell (1982) report that the little girl feels strengthened in father's arms. She sees girls as reworking the separation from mother and utilizing the resurrection of their phallic selves to do this. Her poetic examples articulate the necessity for identification with the male as an ongoing developmental issue. This would be a replay of early childhood.

Oliner (1982), discussing the girl's use of the father in her struggle with the "anal" mother (the instinctual formulation of aspects of the separation struggles), highlights some of the difficulties the girl herself brings to this effort, in addition to the "unlike" issue I have mentioned. She describes the girl's turn to the father as a need to wrest power from him (his penis), in order to have strength to do battle with the omnipotent, controlling mother of the anal phase. Wresting his idealized power (penis) from him then burdens the relationship to him with terrible guilt. This theft and her guilt toward him then make it impossible for her to turn toward him as an erotic object. One of the difficulties in this formulation is in interpreting the girl's need for her father in terms of his penis—a return to a part-object relationship. Indeed, a girl would feel guilty if the only way she could free herself from her mother would be to rob her father of his penis. Nevertheless, elements of this can well enter as impediments to forming adaptive identifications with her father; if it has been an active fantasy, it can interfere as well with her erotic relationship with him.

To the extent that this is an active fantasy—"I have stolen daddy's penis to control mother"—it can mobilize intense guilt toward both parents that impedes resolution of the oedipal or genital crisis. If the relationship with mother remains under the influence of rageful control, core feminine identifications cannot reemerge for building a feminine genital self. The relationship with the father can be burdened by guilt and rage toward the paternal penis that gives him prerogatives with mother, as well as by guilt over wresting it from him.

Chasseguet-Smirgel (1970), in discussing this developmental difficulty, suggests that this kind of trouble leads to the girl who, out of guilt, renounces sexual and autonomous strivings and places herself at "men's service," as right hand or nurse, for example, as endless compensation for the rageful, possessive use of the father's penis.

Electra sounds this theme. She is the devoted, adoring, sexless daughter, an adult version of the good little girl, neat, clean, toilet-trained, and desexualized. She devotes herself to her father's care. Seidenberg and Papathomopoulos (1962) describe this daughter as one who replaces mother, one who can hide from the real relationship to a man, one who through her power as nurse to the ill old man takes hostile revenge on the dominator. They see this position as one into which the girl is forced by an exploitative father who demands and expects that she sacrifice herself. While Electra nurses only her father's memory, she does live with an older man, sleeps with him, but has no sex. The Electra character can be recognized in the character of Antigone, as well as in Balzac's *The Old Maid,* in his *Père Goriot,* in which the father ties his daughters to him after his wife's death, and in his *Eugenie Grandet,* in which the father imprisons his daughter, who then nurses him and later marries without sexually consummating the marriage, thus remaining true to her father.

While there are certainly men who renounce sexuality, it is not a common ego ideal, as is the self-sacrificing, sexually pure daughter who devotes her life to her father (boss or cause). I consider sustained, overt sexual renunciation to be a particularly female response.

Father's absence appears to promote these pathological fantasies and impede the girl's development; this seems to be true whether the father is physically absent or emotionally absent. Absences lead to splitting in a variety of combinations. Mother can be all evil, and the absent father idealized; mother can be all good, and the absent father the repositor of all evil. The absent father can be the container of all aggression and sexuality, leaving the girl unable to negotiate relationships with him or other men. Neubauer (1960) found disturbances along these lines in studying the effects of the absent father. The longer the absence, the more severe was the pathology; the pathology seemed to move to two extremes — either toward oversexualized or overly uncomfortable, inhibited behavior.

Electra, prototypically perched at the entrance to genitality, is immobilized. Father is not present as a source of strength or identification, nor to rescue her from mother or confirm her femininity. She is alone with the preoedipal mother, unable to separate, unable to regress, unable to progress. She is helplessly unable to integrate her sexuality.

Fathers are important to their children from the beginning of their lives. One of the reasons for this can be heard in Electra's cry for her powerful father, "O what perversion, when the woman in the house stands out as master, not the man" (Euripides, *Electra,* ll. 932–933, p. 225). Electra gives no reason why this is a perversion. Her complaints against her mother are endless, though: she is making babies, which makes Electra "shake with hate"; she gives her love to lovers, not her children; she is beautiful; she controls the house, the country, the wealth, Electra's very life. With her father gone, and her stepfather weak and uninterested in her, she is left alone to struggle with her mother. Electra yearns for her father to master mother. His absence allows mother to retain omnipotence in the child's experience.

In summary, the girl's oedipal crisis is quite different from the boy's. The danger to her body is primary, in the fulfillment of her longings. As in earlier stages, her resolutions are more object embedded. Identifications with her father must take place early to establish and maintain individuation. This relationship, including identifications, allows her to identify with mother, including erotically, with safety.

I have not, in this chapter, stressed the rivalries and dangers with mother that are well enough documented and parallel the boy's experience. I have tried to focus on those issues that are very different and make it inaccurate to call the female genital phase "oedipal." Her conflicts and dangers are not the same; her successful mastery is not the same. Electra, who feels helpless and immobilized, who renounces sexuality and remains in isolated, erotic mourning, seems a more appropriate model for girls than Oedipus.

6

Gender Specific Dangers in the Female/Female Dyad in Treatment

There is no substantiated evidence that the gender of the therapist determines the outcome of treatment, whether it be brief, goal-oriented or a long-term classical psychoanalysis. There are many impressions and convictions, and a few traditions. The classical analytical position is that there is no difference; in an analysis, all significant transferences will emerge if the analyst permits and facilitates their emergence.

In general, women have been thought of as more patient, more able to deal with preoedipal material with sicker patients; male colleagues have often referred unsuccessful or stalemated cases to women, in the belief that their more nurturant capacities may bring more success. There have always been women who would seek treatment only with a female therapist, manifestly because they felt they could not reveal embarrassing secrets to a man, or that a woman would automatically understand them. Some have felt they would successfully deceive a man, a variation of "faking it" (Person 1983). There has been a theoretical stance that all patients

who seek women therapists are attempting to work out
unresolved problems with their mothers (Goz 1973). (For
fuller discussion of these positions, see Kalinich 1981, Mogul
1982, Person 1983.)

In today's world, women patients seem to be seeking
women therapists in increasing numbers; this is very different from only a decade ago. The reasons given by these
women are familiar to most of us and have been elaborated
vociferously in much feminist criticism of classical psychoanalytic theory. It is ironic that psychoanalysis, which has
had such a profound influence on the social mores of
contemporary society, such a freeing impact on the lives of
women, should at the same time be viewed as reactionary by
many of today's women seeking treatment.

From my experience with women seeking treatment, one
of their primary reasons for seeking a female therapist at this
point in time, then, is not to have the therapist interpret in
the direction of helping the woman adjust to (that is, accept)
her femininity. Those who are more sophisticated will spell it
out: "I don't want to be told my problem is penis envy."
Karme (1981) has given an exemplary case study of this type
of woman. A second reason given by women is that they
want to have a professional woman with whom they can
identify, often citing their mothers as traditional housewives
living lives that they do not wish to repeat. There is an
implicit assumption that a woman therapist will identify
with, and support their career strivings. There also is often
an implicit assumption that the female therapist is in agreement with the position that men are oppressors, interested in
retaining their position of power and inherently unable to
support such strivings in their women patients.

It would be fairly easy to take one of two positions with
regard to the manifest presentation of motives. One could,
on one hand, take every one of the patient's statements at

face value and treat them as reality. The other would be to see all the patient's statements as defensive, against unresolved conflicts with the mother, or unresolved conflicts with men. As in all treatments, it is important to maintain a perspective on both the reality and the personal meaning of that reality.

ANALYSTS' VULNERABILITIES

Whether the influences on the analyst have their source in the cultural ambiance, such as the Women's Movement (Turkel 1976), in personal goals and values, or in private biographic conflicts, there seem to be gender-specific vulnerabilities that women analysts must confront in order to facilitate most fully the analytic process. (See also Tower 1956, Zetzel 1970.) The female analyst is at risk in analyzing female patients just as much as male analysts are, although the dangers are different. First, many of us are confronted with a natural identification with women's strivings toward autonomy, independence, careers. From this position, we are in danger of failing to analyze the defensive nature involved in such strivings and hence, may leave major conflictual areas untouched. Second, we are in danger of overidentifying with women's complaints about men, whether they be fathers, husbands, bosses, or professors. Often the products of a male-dominated world and male-dominated theory, we may ourselves be too quick to take up the angry stance. Again, our failure would come in not analyzing the feelings of helplessness, frustration, and anger aroused in adult women that have their genesis in childhood conflicts for both analyst and analysand. Failure to be alert can provide a dangerous source of resistance, again for both analyst and analysand.

A third danger that exists is the overvaluation of professional career strivings and a lack of appreciation and respect for the more traditional feminine strivings in our patients. Over the last five to ten years, I have found increasingly that women are ashamed to find out how much they enjoy mothering. When the three-month or six-month leave of absence is over, and the time has come to return to their jobs, often they do not want to leave their babies and go back to work. They feel they are betraying the new woman ideal; it is in this realm that the feminist movement has sadly become antifeminist. Transferentially, women feel they are betraying me, or our "pact," or are a disappointment. These reactions must be analyzed in the transference as a variation of the maternal theme "mother expects me to be just like her."

A fourth danger lies in direct parallel to the male analyst's vulnerability: as the male analyst cannot perceive himself as feminine, the female analyst has most difficulty recognizing when the woman patient sees her as masculine. Here, I am not referring to character attributes such as activity or assertiveness in the woman analyst contrasted to holding, nurturing qualities in the male analyst. The male analyst can experience himself as feminine in the holding aspects, but rarely can he see or experience himself as feminine in the sense of "being penetrated." We women often cannot understand ourselves as "penetrating." Since this can be such a central fear in women and such a common transference experience, it is the one we most often miss, or recognize late.

Another danger that we face is the countertransference issue of awakened competitiveness. This operates in two ways. First, there are feelings of comparison and competition aroused (and actively stimulated, to be sure) by our women patients. Second, our competitiveness with our own mothers is rearoused and directed toward the patient's mother. By definition, I think there is an underlying fantasy in many analysts, male or female, that "we are going to do it better."

A related danger I will touch on here is that of homosexuality. Often one can find oneself identifying with how bad mother was, in the same way one may be seduced into believing how bad father was; in each case we must be aware that this posture really may be masking far more threatening erotic feelings.

The last danger I will take up is that of regression. Clearly, the analysis will lead us into stormy, dangerous regressions — dangerous because these regressions are simultaneously more ego syntonic for women and at the same time pose a greater threat. A delicate balance must be maintained by the analyst between facilitating the regression, on the one hand, and remembering that the regression is in the service of progression, on the other. The predilection for focusing on the mother–daughter relationship is secured by the feminist movement and by recent psychoanalytic theoretical preoccupation. While this complex relationship is significant to an analysis, remaining with this material for long periods can serve as resistance (by both analyst and analysand). I have found regressions in women to be one of the most powerful resistances: by holding onto this position, and by our permitting it, anxieties that must be faced for growth to take place can be deferred unduly.

Clearly, all of the dangers that I have outlined can and do appear in variation in every analysis. While the literature on the gender of the analyst has stressed the patient's reactions, there is an immediacy of empathy in the analyst when confronted with a same gender patient as well. There are gender-specific, particular anxieties that resonate deeply and automatically.

The female/female dyad is, in my opinion, particularly

vulnerable because the gender of both repeats the original dyad. The very gender difference of either patient or analyst in any male/female combination protects both from some of the most archaic, dangerous, and, at the same time, potentially most healing conflicts.

CLINICAL DOCUMENTATION

I would like to illustrate some of these issues with case material, both reported by other analysts, and from some of the cases with which I have worked.

The first example is of a woman seeking a woman therapist for the manifest purpose of working on her relationship to her mother.

Thirty years old, a mother of a 4-month-old daughter, she left her previous female therapist because the patient feared that as a single woman, she couldn't possibly understand the patient's severe depression, or the burdens of motherhood. The patient presented a picture of utter despair, weeping session after session, "I want my Mommy, I want to be a baby, not have one." She reported being obsessed with ideas of the death of her baby and herself and of sleeplessness (among other phobic-like symptoms). Sessions were filled with laments about the miserable condition of the world and the futility of trying to raise a child safely. The current state of child abuse revelations in the news proved to her how unsafe it was to leave her baby for a moment, even to come to sessions.

Convinced that this patient was in a defensive regression, I took a very firm stance that her total preoccupation was symptomatic and actively invited her to wonder why she was "depressed" at a time she anticipated being most happy. As part of this strategy, I asked her when these thoughts seemed to come to her most. She brightened considerably and reported that she was free of them most of the day when she enjoyed her baby daughter immensely, but the second she got into bed alone at night, she became overwhelmed with sadness.

Following this session, the patient had the following dream: "I am here in your office. Instead of you being in here waiting for me, I am in here waiting for you. Suddenly the door flings open wide and Dracula, with his cape spread wide, appears in the room."

In associations, she revealed that her father had been born in Transylvania. The previous therapist, though single, was clearly more nurturant and supportive of the woman's terror of mothering based on what the patient reported to be a terrible deficit in mothering by her own mother. The focus on the maternal aspects detracted from the intense erotic, guilt-ridden, masochistic relationship with her father, whose baby she had just borne (in her unconscious, of course) and for which she was to be punished by death. The oedipal aspects were being defended against by the preoedipal preoccupations. (For a full discussion of the female Oedipus complex, see Chapter 5.)

It is my impression that the former female therapist was overidentified with the "deprived," unmothered child and, simultaneously, was in competition with the patient's mother — dangers inherent in the female/female dyad.

I will give two examples of the differences gender can make in the direction of our interpretive work. The first is from my own practice and centers on the "snake" dream that was presented by a 35-year-old woman. The reader will recall this dream from Chapter 3, where it was discussed in the context of understanding genital anxieties. Here I will review this clinical material from the viewpoint of the dyad, that is, the listening analyst. The patient dreamed that there was a snake in her apartment. She was scared and didn't know where it was, fearing that it would touch her. There was a woman psychologist in a wheelchair but the patient was not sure she could help, since she had some kind of disability or illness. This dream was reported during a time when I was teaching, and I presented it to the class as an example. Every male in the class understood the dream to indicate that the patient saw me, the analyst, as castrated. Some women also saw this aspect; others focused on her distrust of me, reflecting early mother–child difficulties, issues of basic trust.

I saw this material differently. The patient's associations included being taken by surprise, not knowing what was going on. I saw this as reflecting her anxiety over where her own sexuality resided and how she could locate and gain control over it — an early problem girls must face (and which I have dealt with in Chapter 3). I interpreted the dream as follows. She was frightened to have her husband touch her sexually (material that had opened the session and been presented to the class), and she was worried whether I, as a woman, whom she saw as a weak, disabled creature (she saw women as weak generally), would be capable, able to help her with her fear. Her fear focused on the fact that she didn't know where it (the snake, and sexuality) was. In short, I focused on her anxiety about mastery — both in herself and in me. The patient, who had been quite depressed, inert, bored, and listless, came in the next session with the first bright smile I'd seen in our two years of work, and with a twinkle told me of a sudden renewed interest in the stock market, of some trades she had made in the intervening day, of her contemplating buying a seat on a new market exchange that was opening that she would control, renting it to others who wanted to trade (her space that she could rent out to men for money). Her movement was clearly to a position in which she did not feel helpless, but could control, manipulate, and enjoy. In terms of the transference, the important point is that to have focused on her perception of me as castrated and disabled, or on problems of basic trust would have put the two of us together in a hopeless heap and would, I think, have been an intellectualization for the patient or confirmation of her worst fears. She was afraid of sex. Would I be able to help her with this scary sex that she couldn't see, and that could dart out from anywhere (the inherent invisibility of her genitals)? To have focused on her fear of her husband's genitals would have been incorrect (or incomplete); her anxieties over her own genitals were involved. Her anxiety was over how she could have control over herself as well as her husband. This vignette illustrates the way in which classic theory can shape our listening and may cause us to miss important material.

My own overidentification with a woman patient caused her to flee treatment with me. She was pregnant for the third time, having terminated two earlier pregnancies in abortion, but this time expressed considerable longing to keep the pregnancy and have a child, a position resulting from our previous work together. When her husband again opposed the pregnancy and demanded that she again have an abortion, I actively encouraged her determined stance to hold onto her wishes in opposition to her husband. This was a position that this woman never took, always finding some rationalization for agreeing with him, even when her initial feelings were clearly different. Shortly after this, she got into an intense negative transference resistance, didn't want to see me anymore, or talk to me anymore, based on some disagreement over policy. She later entered treatment with a respected colleague and I had the opportunity to inquire if the reasons for her interruption of our work had emerged. When my colleague told me the woman felt I had taken such a strong position in relation to the pregnancy that she felt helpless to express her own real ambivalence, I realized immediately that she was accurate. I suspect when we find ourselves that angry with our patients' men, we had better look inside a bit before intervening.

Person (1983) gives an example of the influence of values on interpretation. A female patient, in treatment with a male therapist, felt that her depression resulted from being home with her children; she was withdrawn, and felt isolated and unable to form intimate ties, despite loving feelings. Her marriage was deteriorating. She decided to return to work, in the hope of reviving self-esteem that would allow her to be more functional at home. Her male therapist interpreted her intent as acting out and a defense against closeness with her children and as the wish to abandon them. She fell into a silent rage and Person was consulted by the male therapist. Person and the therapist agreed that the patient was attempting to break a negative identification with her own mother, precipitated by staying at home. They understood that the patient felt the therapist's interpretation was an indictment that she was as unable to give as her mother had been; she was no good. This led to the increase in depression, guilt, and withdrawal. Person saw the patient's plan differently, as an adaptive maneuver.

I would have probably agreed with Person at this point — that the disidentification from a depressed mother must take place. However, at some point, perhaps after some integration of differentiation, this woman must address her conflicts in expressing love in her family. It is, however, an exemplary case of how women's therapies have suffered biases. The move toward professional involvement is often interpreted, as this male therapist did, as a flight from femininity, and not as an attempt at mastery or autonomy, a step that must be taken for true femininity and integration of mothering to evolve (see Chapter 4).

McDougall (1986), in her willingness to reveal her personal vulnerabilities, reports an outstanding example of a countertransference stance, one that I think may be common among us. It includes issues of competitiveness, envy, and homoeroticism. (I am excerpting from a longer presentation.) Her analysand, Madame T, complained bitterly about her mother's "overwhelming . . . solicitude by which she claimed to be persecuted. . . . her mother would seize any slim pretext to get her daughter home, as though she were constantly replaiting the umbilical cord in a symbolic attempt to draw her phobic child back into her womb. Invitations to dine, to stay for the weekend, or to accompany the parents to the theater were rained upon Madame T" (p. 223). McDougall continues, " 'A real cannibal mother,' I thought to myself, 'and perverse as well! Not only does she complain that her daughter has been neurotically crippled for the past thirty years, but she also does everything in her power to keep her in this state!' " (p. 223). During the session that preceded McDougall's insight, the patient had stated that her night terrors had ended, but that the daytime ones were as strong as ever; she then described an extreme reaction to visiting the home of an older woman friend. McDougall was not pleased with the work of the session, which seemed empty and repetitive; then she had a dream. She adds that she, like her patient, was sleeping alone that night. The dream: "I . . . find myself in the presence of a very attractive Oriental woman, dressed in a provocative, sexy style. . . . I stammer out some sort of excuse [for being late] and reach forward to caress the silken material of her dress, as though to be forgiven or to be seductive to her. It becomes evident that I am to have an erotic relationship with this lady . . . [but] I am not sure what is expected of me. . . . I am then convinced that I must . . . passively submit to whatever this beautiful woman wants" (p. 225). To condense an elegant account, the Oriental woman had been seen in consultation; her name was Lili. McDougall's mother's name was Lillian. Her exploration led her to realize that her own mother was the opposite of Madame T's mother—busy, undemanding toward her daughters. She then proceeded to find she was envious of Madame T's possessive mother. "Why did I not have a mother like that," she mused (p. 226). She had analyzed all the hostile feelings in herself and her patient, but she had

overlooked the "supreme importance of [Madame T's] positive feelings and her homosexual attachment to her mother,
because of [her own] need to keep in repression [her] own
childlike wish to be the chosen subject of [her] mother's
erotic desire" (p. 226). Two analyses with men had not
uncovered this material.

I think this not uncommon, in that erotic feeling toward a
male analyst can so swiftly be seen as oedipal. After her
insight, she opened the issue with Madame T and the analysis
proceeded to reveal that the demanding one was really the
patient herself and not the mother. It was the mother who
yearned to be with her husband without her daughter ever
present. Chasseguet-Smirgel (1984) has addressed some of
these issues. She sees the female dyad as potentially dangerous, in terms of regression, but sees the analytic situation as
the protector. "In its role as boundary, the [analytic] setting
is law, a cut-off point, a representative of the father" (p.
176). The analytic situation both induces and allows the
regression and, simultaneously, opposes it, limiting it,
binding it, and protecting the patient and analyst from it.
She presents a dream that she considers typical of the woman
therapist: "It is morning. The analyst is arranging her
consulting room ready to receive a patient. But her mother,
or a substitute, intervenes and by her actions prevents the
room from being put in order. The couch is a bed which has
to be remade and have a cover put on it, but the mother stays
there and, for various reasons, impedes the daughter's work;
or else the mother has left some underclothes or her night-
dress lying around on the furniture; or else she hangs around
in the room and refuses to leave, etc." (p. 176).

Chasseguet-Smirgel sees the dream as an expression of
what is mobilized in us by the exercise of our profession, the
fundamental bisexuality of the human being—maternity on
the one hand and the legislative character of the paternal

phallus on the other. In the dream, the mother "is the instigator of excitation, prevents desexualization and thus inhibits the functioning of the analyst's thought processes" (p. 176). In order to do our work, we must be able to utilize the conflicting forces of both components, the male and female self.

THE EMERGENCE OF GENITAL ANXIETIES IN DYADIC INTERACTION

These I see as difficulties rooted in developmental issues for both the female analyst and analysand. In the preceding chapters, I have attempted to describe feminine development as different from, and not an aberrant form of, male development—a view that has dominated our theory since Freud's formulations, placing the oedipal situation and castration at the center of development.

I have defined female genital anxieties as specific to female genitalia and attempted to trace their role in female development. Here I will briefly review them and relate these formulations to the dyad difficulties outlined, illustrated by Chasseguet-Smirgel's material.

I have described three clusters of anxieties in the female—access, penetration, and diffusivity. These anxieties stem from the nature of the female genitalia, as castration stems from the nature of male genitals. The inaccessibility of female genitals through normal sensory modes—sight, touch, as well as specificity of sensation—creates difficulties in forming mental representations of critical parts of her body. This occurs during the toddler phase of development, when issues of differentiation and self-definition are the central developmental tasks. The phase is also saturated with issues of control—over the body in terms of developing musculature and anal control, with the mother in terms of autonomy, with the world in terms of language acquisition and symbol formation.

Lacking the sensory modes of body mastery, girls rely far more on their mothers (and their fathers) for mastery of these central developmental tasks. For help in mastering the diffusivity emanating from her own genital experience, the girl must turn to mother; yet her turn to mother for mastery also reawakens the diffusivity of the early undifferentiated relationship with her. Where is her genital? She must trust mother's assurance that it is tucked away. How can she control access and penetration to an opening that has no sphincter? She must learn to say "no," itself fraught with conflict between mother and daughter. Each of these illustrates the ongoing embeddedness of the girl's development — it must all be worked out within the context of the maternal tie.

This formulation gives clinical psychoanalytic understanding to the long-noted object connectedness in women. Freud (1926) pointed us in this direction quite clearly in "Inhibitions, Symptoms and Anxiety," where he described the boy's central anxiety as castration and the girl's (having already been castrated) as "loss of love of the object" (p. 143). Freud did not elaborate the impact of such a formulation. He defines boys' concerns as more narcissistic, in terms of their bodies, and defines girls' as more object embedded.

The problems that I have described and illustrated in the clinical situation of the female/female dyad have their roots in these developmental conflicts. The flight from mothering has its roots in the early flight from mother. The intricate balance of identification and disidentification that must take place is fraught for all girls, whether the mother was depressed or not, as in Person's case (1983) described previously. The use of the outer world of work, usually identified with father, has become an extension of the identification with father that helps girls differentiate. My 30-year-old patient and her former therapist were involved in a regressive, sticky mother/child transference in addition to the mother/analyst competitiveness, and it took the fresh air of introducing the conflicts with her father to help her out of her depression. My patient who dreamed of the snake was struggling with issues of control that impaired her sense of self and self-esteem and made it impossible to relate safely to her husband, until she could take control over her own body. (Her brothers were stockbrokers, by the way.) McDougall's description is self-evident: the early erotic tie to the mother was being protected from emergence, analysis, and integration by the continued mobilization of anger. Chasseguet-Smirgel's description illustrates very vividly the regressive dangers to both analyst and analysand.

The daughter, now analyst, must extricate herself from the regressive and sexual aspects of her relationship with her mother. She must integrate the different, body alien, ordering aspects of her father into her psyche, and into her professional work. This requires the female, most particularly as analyst, to be able to move back and forth with safety and flexibility between regressive, erotic, intuitive modes, and intellectual, curious, truly analytic modes, often within a single hour.

7

On Cinderella*

EDITOR'S INTRODUCTION (B. D.)

Doris Bernstein first presented her thoughts about Cinderella in a workshop at the Spring meetings of the American Psychological Association, Division 39, in 1985. At that time, she explained how she had come to reread the tales.

In writing her paper on the female Oedipus complex, she had discussed the myth of Electra; but she had come to the conclusion that Electra's relationship with her mother was mired in preoedipal issues, exacerbated by her absent father, and that Electra failed to achieve full oedipal resolution. Mrs. Bernstein was searching for an image for successful feminine oedipal development. In her search, Antigone, too, was considered, but Antigone remained at the level of loving devotion to her family and failed to achieve integration of

---

*Doris Bernstein and Betsy Distler

159

her sexuality. Doris Bernstein then turned from the Greek myths to fairy tales.

The idea of Cinderella came to her out of her clinical work. In the course of listening to her female patients, she noticed that two common identity themes emerged: one had to do with being a Cinderella, the other with being a princess. She spent some months reading and researching the myriad versions of the Cinderella tale. What she was surprised to discover was that there were not two distinct identity themes, but that this one heroine evolved within her own tale from a Cinderella type, as it were, into a princess. The Cinderella she discovered bore no resemblance to the popular Disney character, nor to the stereotypic masochist. Nor is this Cinderella a story only of women, as perhaps one has tended to think, because of Perrault's familiar version of the tale. As the Brothers Grimm tell the tale, Cinderella's use of what she gets from her father to help her on her journey toward maturity is of crucial importance. And that journey is from a dyadic relationship with her mother to the triadic oedipal relationships.

* * * *

TWO CINDERELLAS

The current popular view of Cinderella as a masochist would seem to derive from the version of the tale published by Charles Perrault in 1697. This was already a fairly late permutation, since the tale is the oldest recorded folk tale, the earliest written versions of which date to 9th-century China. The tale had already evolved by that time and, one speculates, changed in the course of oral transmission. As it spread through diffusion of the story plots to the Near East and into Europe, it was altered and enriched with details that reflected the local mores, values, and traditions.

Pretty and Sweet (Perrault)

In writing his version for the French court, Perrault, too, altered the tale. He simplified and prettified both the story and the heroine and removed all unpleasantness. From the very beginning, Perrault makes it clear who is good and who is evil—the stepmother being "the proudest and most haughty woman that was ever seen," and her "two daughters of her own humor," while Cinderella is "of unparalleled goodness and sweetness of temper, which she took from her mother, who had been the best creature in the world" (Perrault 1697, p. 16). Perrault describes everything in such terms, whether good and evil or splendor and wretchedness. We are told that while the stepmother made Cinderella work to the bone as her own daughters preened themselves and rested, Cinderella bore all this patiently, daring not to tell her father because this wife "governed him entirely" (p. 16). Predictably, when the stepsisters were invited to the ball given by the King's son, it was Cinderella who worked hard to prepare their clothes—dressing them perfectly—and who also gave them advice—for the best, always. In this tale, Cinderella accepts her plight. When asked by her stepsisters, "Would you not be glad to go to the ball?" she replies, "Alas! You only jeer me; it is not for such as I am to go thither!" (p. 17). After days of helping them prepare, when the stepsisters leave for the ball, Cinderella collapses in tears. The fairy godmother appears, asking what is the matter. Cinderella can only get as far as "I wish I could . . ." (p. 17) before her tears and sobbing take over. It is the fairy godmother who articulates Cinderella's wish to go to the ball, and it is she who equips her to go, with magically transformed pumpkin/ coach, mice/horses, and so forth. The extent of Cinderella's contribution to her salvation consists in fetching the pumpkin and mice, and thinking to fetch a rat to be transformed into the requisite coachman. She also reminds the fairy godmother, "Must I go thither as I am, in these nasty rags?" (p. 18) and thereby gets the requisite gold and silver ball gown and glass slippers—all via magic, by the good graces of the fairy godmother.

Cinderella is greeted upon her arrival at the ball by the King's son, who was told a great princess had come whom no one knew. The music and dancing stop as she enters, as everyone contemplates her singular beauties and the ladies especially, her clothes and headdress, so that they might have the same made for themselves the next day.

Perrault tells us that Cinderella "went and sat down by her sisters, showing them a thousand civilities, giving them part of the oranges and citrons which the Prince had presented her with" (p. 19).

Cinderella returns home before midnight, thanks her fairy godmother, and tells her "she could not but heartily wish she might go next day to the ball, because the King's son had desired her" (p. 19). Note she does not mention any desire of her own. Upon her sisters' return, Cinderella pretends she has been sleeping. The stepsisters tell her of the beautiful princess and her kindness to them. We are told that Cinderella seemed very indifferent in the matter, but she does then come alive, enjoying inquiring who this princess is. When she is told that the King's son "would give all the world to know who she is," Cinderella smiles and asks: "Could I not see her?" (p. 20). And she asks one of her stepsisters to lend her some everyday clothes so she might go. She is, predictably, rebuffed—to her relief! She does attend the next day's ball, of course (with the same magical help), "dressed more magnificently than before" (p. 20). Enjoying the Prince's compliments and attention, Cinderella forgets to leave; when suddenly the clock strikes midnight, she flees. The Prince rushes after her and picks up the glass slipper that she has left behind. All that remains of her fine garments when she reaches home is the remaining glass slipper. Her sisters return and report about the ball—about the beautiful princess's sudden departure at midnight, and the certainty that the Prince is in love with "the beautiful person who owned the glass slipper" (p. 21).

A few days later, the Prince proclaims his intent to marry the woman whose foot the slipper fits. When the slipper is brought to Cinderella's home, her sisters "did all they possibly could to thrust their foot into the slipper, but they could not effect it" (p. 21). Cinderella watches, then suggests they see if it will fit her. The sisters laugh at the idea, but the gentleman has a sense of duty and lets her try; the slipper fits Cinderella exactly. She pulls the other slipper out of her pocket and puts it on. Enter the fairy godmother, who waves her wand to change Cinderella's rags into an even more splendid outfit than before. The stepsisters throw themselves at Cinderella's feet and beg forgiveness for all their ill treatment of her. Cinderella embraces and forgives them. She is brought to the Prince, who marries her a few days later. And the story concludes: "Cinderella, who was no less good than beautiful, gave her two sisters lodgings in the palace, and that very same day matched them with two great lords of the court" (p. 21).

Thus Perrault's tale is one of the triumph of goodness. The heroine succeeds because of her inherent goodness: forces of magic materialize in response to her wishes. Neither ingenuity nor action are displayed by her—no obstacles for her to overcome, no tasks by which to prove herself, no outwitting of evil forces. Only patience, passivity, and beauty comprise her heroism.

Perrault's simplified Cinderella is a tale of women. One is struck by the father's absence. There is no separate, different "other" to help the girl in her development from a dependent child to an independent existence, from nonsexual drabness to resplendent, sexual young-womanhood, from helpless victim to confident victor. She would remain an ineffectual little child wishing for magic to undo her sorry position, unable to move on in her life, were it not for the arrival of magical transformations as a reward for her own superior "goodness" (as defined by Perrault – that is, cheerful acceptance of her plight).

Cinderella's good cheer is indeed striking, with an absence of revenge fantasies toward her stepmother and stepsisters. The rage that would be appropriate to someone in her position is turned into attempts at self-control; via reaction formation, she becomes super good, super helpful. She forgives their horrid behavior toward her; she "embraced them, cried that she forgave them with all her heart, and desired them always to love her" (p. 21). It is this that could be viewed as the basis for Berliner's (1947) calling Cinderella an example of a simple form of masochism – like the dog who becomes more devoted and loving the more he is beaten. Berliner (1947) termed masochism not an instinct – sadism turned upon the self, out of guilt or a need for punishment – as Freud had written, but a character neurosis, a "defense mechanism of the ego against an instinctual conflict" (p. 460). It occurs when the child has received hostile treatment from its love objects; the hostility is denied, and the pain-giving object is introjected, out of the child's need for love in order to survive. Thus at the hands of her hostile stepmother and siblings, Cinderella "responds . . . with humble devotion." She "knew that she was good and loving, and had the undying hope in her heart that one day she would be rewarded" According to Berliner, "suffering enhances the individual's sense of his value as a love object, and he may therefore feel good" (p. 462).

Berliner's and Perrault's masochistic Cinderella fits well into the early psychoanalytic conception of the "normal" feminine character. Freud postulated a normal feminine masochism, an intrinsic element of woman's constitution, based in her inevitable disappointment in her genital and, by extension, in her mother. Her turning from mother to father is in search of compensation for the penis she lacks, and she is required to fantasize passive submission to father in order to acquire the longed for penis/child. Her acceptance of her gender is seen as masochistic resignation.

Deutsch (1925), expanding upon Freud, saw the female genital as heir to the oral zone: the vagina takes over the role of the mouth in the passive-oral function of suckling. Just as the mother's breast invested libido in the mouth, so it is the penis that invests libido in the vagina. The vagina is, then, only discovered in sexual relations. In childbirth, the vagina becomes the container for the child, which in the unconscious the penis represents. Here the woman gives up the claim of the clitoris to represent the penis, allowing the vagina to assume the maternal function, and she reaches the ultimate goal of female development: for the act of parturition is the height of sexual pleasure — masochistic pleasure, since it entails pain. For Deutsch, then, as for Freud, passivity (submission) and masochism are seen to define femininity.

But subsequent developments in psychoanalytic theory and deepened understanding of the once dark continent of the female psyche have brought about reformulations. (For a full discussion of these developments in psychoanalytic

theory, see Fliegel 1986.) Of particular importance is the
shift from the early view of femininity as a secondary,
compensatory state to the understanding of a primary femininity (Stoller 1976); in this view, masochism becomes no
longer an inevitable component of female character but a
sometime residue of unresolved conflict. The woman's
ability to tolerate pain (childbirth, etc.) must be differentiated from a masochistic wish for pain. So, too, the capacity
to make self-sacrifices (as, for instance, in caring for her
children) must be viewed as a pleasurable living up to an ego
ideal, not as an expression of masochism.

Forceful and Resourceful (Grimm)

With this shift in understanding comes a search for a new
model. Having noted that Perrault's Cinderella was but the
beginning of one trend in the tale's evolution (the culmina-
tion of which in America is the insipid Disney version), we
now turn to the tradition of Cinderella tales in which the
heroine actively struggles to get what she wants. This tradition—forming the bulk of the seven hundred or so known
Cinderella variations—might well provide us with a model of
the young woman struggling to move forward in her own
development to a mature femininity in which genital sexuality is integrated.

The best known example is the one recorded by the
Brothers Grimm in 1812, entitled "Aschenputtel," or "Ash
Girl." Prominent in this tale, as in the many others of its
type, is Cinderella's beginning as a beloved and privileged
child. (This is already counter to the early environmental
sadism postulated by Berliner [1947] in his account of the
origins of masochism.) In some versions of the tale, a point
is made of the father's love for his daughter, and that her

love gives her great power over him, that she could get him to do anything she wished. Grimm tells us, "a rich man's wife fell ill and, feeling that her end was approaching, called her only daughter to her bedside and said, 'Dear child, remain devout and good; then dear God will ever be with you, and I'll look down on you from Heaven and be near you'" (Grimm and Grimm 1812, p. 23). After she died, the girl went daily to her mother's grave and wept, and she remained devout and good as her mother had wished. A year later, the father remarried. "The wife brought two daughters of her own into the home," who were "pretty and fair of face but ugly and black in their hearts" (p. 24). At this point, the father practically disappears from every story, and "evil days" begin for the "poor stepchild." The stepmother and stepsisters "took away her fine clothes, dressed her in an old gray smock and wooden shoes" (p. 24). It is described how they mocked and insulted her, and how they would lead her into the kitchen, where she had to do heavy work from before dawn until night, carry water, light the fire, cook, and wash. Her sisters played mean tricks on her, poured peas and lentils into the ashes so she'd have to pick them out. She had no bed other than the ashes beside the hearth. And because this made her look dusty and dirty, they called her Ash Girl. In none of the tales is there a reason given for this behavior toward a pleasant child. Nor is Ash Girl in any way wanting or provoking such terrible treatment. She is dressed in rags and, in some versions, prohibited from washing and combing. All the while, her stepsisters parade in beautiful clothes that she is forced to sew and iron for them. Yet poor Ash Girl maintains good cheer, works hard, is cooperative and noncomplaining.

One day, the father was going to a fair and asked the girls what they wanted him to bring them. The two sisters said fine clothes and jewels, while Ash Girl told him: " 'Father, bring me the first twig that brushes against your hat on the way home. Break it off for me' " (p. 24). In another variation, she bids him send her regards to a distant fairy, who sends her a sapling with watering can and spade. Grimm tells us, "As he was riding home through a green thicket, a hazel twig brushed against him and knocked off his hat; then he broke off the twig and brought it along. When he got home, he gave his stepdaughters what they'd asked for and gave Ash Girl the hazel twig. She thanked him, went to her mother's grave, planted the twig, and wept so bitterly that her tears fell on it and watered it. It grew and became a fine tree" (p. 24). Some tales describe the tree as grown to the size of a woman. Three times a day, Ash Girl went to her tree, wept and prayed; every time she uttered a wish, a little white bird, lighted on the tree, would throw down to her what she had wished.

One day, the king proclaimed a festival, to last three days, so his son could choose a bride. "All the pretty girls in the land were invited" (p. 24), including the stepsisters, who made Ash Girl help them get ready. Though she obeyed them, she wept, for she would have liked to go along to the ball, and begged her stepmother to let her. " 'You, Ash Girl!' she said, 'you're covered with dust and dirt, and you want to go to the festival? You've got no clothes and no shoes and you want to dance?' " But when Ash Girl persisted, "the stepmother finally said, 'I emptied a dish of lentils in the ashes; if you pick out the lentils within two hours, you may come along' " (p. 25). Ash Girl went into the garden and cried out to her birds to help her. A multitude of birds flew in to help, getting the job done in less than an hour. When she joyfully brought the dish to her stepmother, thinking she might now be allowed to go to the festival, the stepmother said, " 'No, Ash Girl, you've got no clothes and don't know how to dance; you'll only be laughed at.' " Ash Girl wept and was told, " 'If you can pick two dishes of lentils from the ashes in one hour, you may come along' " (p. 25). The stepmother believed it impossible, of course, and emptied the two dishes of lentils into the ashes. Once again Ash Girl went into the garden and cried to the birds for help. They finished "in hardly half an hour," but when she brought the dishes to her stepmother, she met with: " 'It'll do you no good. You're not coming along, for you've got no clothes and don't know how to dance. We'd only be ashamed of you' " (p. 26). With that, Ash Girl went to her mother's grave under the hazel bush and cried to the tree to scatter gold and silver on her. "Then the bird threw her down a gold and silver dress and silk slippers embroidered with silver" (p. 26). She rushed into the clothes and away to the festival, where, unrecognized by her stepmother and stepsisters ("they thought she must be some foreign princess" [p. 26]), she danced with the prince until evening.

When she decided to go home, the prince wanted to escort her — to see whose daughter she was. But "she slipped away from him" and "jumped into the dovecote" (p. 26). At this point, the father reappears (in Grimm as in most versions), for the prince told him what this "foreign girl" had done. "The old man thought, 'Can it be Ash Girl?' They had to fetch him an ax and a pick to break down the dovecote, but there was no one inside" (p. 26). They found Ash Girl at home, lying in the ashes, and we are told that she'd run from the dovecote to the hazel bush, where she'd taken off her fine clothes and laid them on her mother's grave.

The next day, Ash Girl again took herself to the hazel bush to ask for finery, and again she dressed herself in it and went to the festival. The prince again took her by the hand and danced only with her. When she left the festival, this time the prince followed her to see where she lived; but she evaded him by climbing into a big pear tree in the garden behind the house. The prince waited for her father and told him, " 'The stranger slipped away from me, and I think she climbed the pear tree.' The father thought, 'Can it be Ash Girl?' He had an ax fetched and cut down the tree, but there was no one in it" (p. 27). Again, they found Ash Girl in the kitchen, lying in the ashes.

The third day of the festival saw a repetition of the previous days' events, with an even more magnificent dress provided for her and slippers of solid gold. This time when she decided to leave the festival, she quickly got away from the prince so he couldn't follow her (note this girl was faster than the boy!). But he had been crafty and covered the stairs with pitch, trapping her "tiny and dainty" (p. 27) left slipper there. The next morning he went to Ash Girl's father and announced his intent to marry the girl whose foot fit the slipper. The stepsisters, delighted, took turns trying on the slipper. When the elder couldn't get her big toe in, her mother, handing her a knife, advised, " 'Cut the toe off; once you're queen, you won't have to walk any more.' " (p. 28). This accomplished, the prince "took her on his horse as his bride" (p. 28). But as they rode by the hazel bush, the two pigeons cried out that there was blood in the shoe and the right bride was still at home. Having thus been alerted to the bloody shoe, the prince returned and had the other stepsister try. This one succeeded in getting her toes in, but her heel wouldn't fit; and so her mother handed her a knife and the same line of advice. She rode off with the prince until the pigeons noticed the blood and once again alerted the prince. On his return to the house, he commented, " 'She isn't the right bride either . . . Haven't you any other daughter?" The father replies, "No, there's only a little misshapen Ash Girl, daughter by my late wife, but she can't possibly be the bride" (p. 28). When the prince asked for her, the stepmother chimed in, "Oh no, she's much too dirty and mustn't be seen"

(p. 28). But the prince insisted, and so Ash Girl washed her face and hands and came before the prince. The slipper fitted her perfectly. When the prince "looked into her face, he recognized her as the beautiful girl with whom he'd danced and cried, 'That's the right bride!' " (p. 29). The stepmother and stepsisters were horrified but helpless, of course. As the prince and Ash Girl rode by the hazel bush, the pigeons cried out their assurance that this was indeed the right bride; they each perched on one of her shoulders and stayed there.

Came the wedding, "the two false sisters came and wanted to ingratiate themselves and have a share in her good fortune." On the way into the church, the pigeons pecked out an eye of each of the sisters; on the way out, they pecked out the other eye. Grimm ends the tale, "Thus for their malice and treachery they were punished with blindness for the rest of their lives" (p. 29).

Thus in the Grimm and most other versions of the tale, evil is punished, not forgiven, and Cinderella is restored to power and position. Cinderella neither seeks suffering nor renounces her wish to go to the ball. She begs to go, completes the requisite tasks, and, when her environment continues to fail her, she uses her own resourcefulness to achieve what she wants. She remains busy throughout, tending her tree, communicating with her bird friends, and weeping with sadness at her lonely lot — appropriate reactions to her plight.

THE OEDIPAL PHASE THROUGH THE COMPARATIVE STUDY OF MYTH

That a tale survives over so many centuries and finds a place in the hearts of children and adults throughout so many different cultures surely suggests a resonance with something fundamental in human experience. Each area, each age, has particularized the tale, mostly by elaborating details that facilitate an instant identification between listener (or reader) and story. Yet paradoxically perhaps, the more recognizable are the small details to the listener, the more deeply the story is then able to resonate, that is, the universal, fundamental Cinderella experience enters one's deepest awareness. So, too, does the Cinderella tale resonate with our own psychoanalytically informed understanding of that phase of female development that corresponds to the male oedipal phase. Can we draw an analogy, then, between the tale and this understanding?

A comparison of the Grimm Cinderella tale with the Perrault reveals a very different developmental model. Perrault's Cinderella fits the model of the girl's Oedipus as an inversion of the boy's. In this reductionistic view there is no conflict, no struggle between Cinderella and the original, good mother. There is only the "good" Cinderella mistreated by the "bad" (step)mother. She is guilty of no crime. The mistreatment she suffers — the deprivation, the "beating" — is her castration, and she accepts her lot until the time comes when she is restored to "completion" by the arrival of her prince. This is the classic Freudian female Oedipus, with masochism seen as an inevitable aspect of development. To put it most simply, Cinderella's masochistic resignation to her castrated lot, her denigrated position, follows a period of anger and disappointment with her mother (symbolized in the wicked stepmother), who lacks as well as deprives her (step)daughter of a "proper" (i.e., male) genital; out of this disappointment comes a turn to her father.

What is the developmental model suggested by the Grimm tale? We are given a little more information at the beginning of this version about Ash Girl's (Cinderella's) predicament than we are in the Perrault, that Ash Girl was a beloved and privileged child, the only child of a rich man (a little princess, in effect?). Her mother is ill and, knowing that she will die, tells Ash Girl to "remain devout and good" (p. 23). This is the ideal her mother instills in her, which is to become her ego ideal as it were. Mother also assures her that then God will be with her and she, too, will be near her as she watches over her from heaven. Ash Girl does as she is told, going daily throughout the following year to weep at her mother's grave. So far, the story is between Ash Girl and her loving mother; no reference is made to father (unless that can be inferred from the mention of God) until we are told, a year later, that he remarries. This event marks a radical turn in Ash Girl's fortune. For no stated reason, her stepmother and stepsisters take away her finery, force her to do all the work, mock her, and play mean tricks on her—in short, cruelty and sadism reign, and no one is there to stop it. This has been viewed psychoanalytically as the emergence of the girl's rivalrous relationship with her mother, the mother who stands between the girl and her father, frustrating her oedipal longings. In this reading, the death of the beloved mother represents Ash Girl's own rivalrous death wishes toward her. The situation in which Ash Girl finds herself, her sudden loss of place, power, and favor, conveys her feeling of being left out, the nonpreferred child. A child whose father "betrays" her by choosing another woman over her would indeed be hurt and angry enough. Since there is no mention in the tale of such feelings toward the father, one reads some of the wickedness of the stepmother and stepsisters as a projection of Ash Girl's own rage and sadism at both of her real parents, whom she then preserves through idealization (certainly the "dead"—or lost—good mother). The inaccessibility of her father threatens to leave her stuck in a dyadic struggle with her devalued mother, ruled by her own and her mother's sadism.

At this point in the story, one hears echoes of Electra, whose aggression gets bound up in a masochistic impasse, in the absence of her father. Electra competes with her mother for virtue: "Now I am what a slave is . . . while they go proud. . . . And for myself, grant that I be more temperate of heart than my mother; that I act with purer hand. . . . (Aeschylus, ll. 135–141) I am one . . . with no loving husband for champion. . . . I tenant my father's house in the ugly rags and stand at a scanty table" (Sophocles, ll. 186–191).

But unlike Electra, whose masochism becomes her weapon, who renounces sexuality and derives erotic pleasure from her suffering, the Grimms' Ash Girl finds her way out. The turning point in the story—the move toward resolution—occurs, significantly, with the next mention of the father. We are told that he is going to a fair and asks his daughters what they would like him to bring them. While the stepsisters ask for fine clothing and jewels, Ash Girl asks for something we take to symbolize what she needs from him to proceed in her development. She asks him to break off the first twig that brushes against his hat on the way home and bring it to her. What is this gift and what use does she make of it? Ash Girl takes the twig immediately to her mother's grave and plants it there, letting it be watered by her tears. We are told that it grows to become a fine tree; in some tales it is described as grown to the size of a woman. This "phallic" gift from father, planted at mother's grave, serves to resurrect her early, lost good mother in a new form, to be used in new ways. It's being described as grown to the size of a woman suggests that it also serves as a symbol of Ash Girl's growth into a woman. Participating in father's power and nurturing something that grows out of the early mother she has lost seems a lovely metaphor for the process of internalization of both father and mother. She must in fact lose that early mother — she must break that tie — and yet at the same time she must also maintain her connection with mother. The helpful gift from her father enables her to do this. The image of Ash Girl and her tree nicely condenses this important developmental step. Her industriousness — her cleaning, sewing, sweeping — helps her gain the life skills she will need. Her daily graveside prayers, in compliance with her mother's parting behest, suggest an internalization of her ego ideal. These activities and identifications sustain her through this period of isolation (separation).

The next phase of the story opens with the king proclaiming a festival in order for his son to choose a bride. While her stepsisters are invited to attend, the stepmother forbids Ash Girl to go, telling her she does not have what it takes ("You've got no clothes and no shoes and you want to dance?" [p. 25]). The prohibiting mother excludes Ash Girl from the social/sexual scene. How does Ash Girl deal with this? She begs to go, persisting until she is in effect told that she must first prove herself. Certain tasks are presented to her that she must master. She must sort the (desirable) lentils from the (dirty, unwanted) ashes her stepmother has mixed with them. What might be the meaning of this need to attain mastery at this juncture of her development? We know that the move toward genitality brings with it anxiety over body integrity — fears of diffusivity, anxiety, and confusion about access, for example (see Chapter 3) — so Ash Girl must develop a sense of clarity and mastery over her body, including differentiation of her genital from the anal and urethral functions. The sorting she is asked to do seems a nice metaphor for this task.

Ash Girl needs help and turns to her good mother, in the form of her bird friends who live in her tree. With this help, she gets the job done. But her stepmother still denies her wish, telling her that she would be laughed at if she were to come with them. Again Ash Girl persists, until she is given a new sorting task, this time twice as many lentils in half the time. Again, she turns to her birds for help, and they finish in even less time than before. When she is again denied the right to go (being told this time that they would only be ashamed of her), she goes to her mother's grave and asks her tree to scatter gold and silver on her. The bird comes forth with a gold and silver outfit, and thus equipped, Ash Girl is off to the ball. She *looks* the part of the beautiful princess, and is chosen by the prince to be his partner.

While the stepmother's exclusionary attitude is clear — the forbidding oedipal mother — this image also represents stages in Ash Girl's own struggle and sense of preparedness. First she herself feels she doesn't have what it takes, and indeed, every little girl measures herself against her mother, whose attributes, capacities, and privileges she wants but can't gain access to. The task of sorting helps her achieve clarity and mastery over her body. But still she is uncertain: she fears she will be laughed at, humiliated in her wish to be grown up, beautiful, and sexual. And so she again patiently sorts, this time achieving a further measure of mastery. Now the remaining fear that resides within her, some glimmer of shame in showing herself, competing, is fought against. She gets help for herself in the form of a resplendent outfit, and she moves out into the competitive world to claim her place, her prince.

But Ash Girl slips away from the prince at the end of the evening; she hides in her dovecote, then returns her fine clothes and retreats to her rags and hearth. She appears to be frightened, not yet ready for this new phase. Competitiveness scares her, and she trades her resplendent gold and silver gown for her old noncompetitive garb. She must achieve something more before she feels ready to claim her place. Again enter her father. The prince asks Ash Girl's father for help in finding her. The father, in a significant move toward restoring her to her position as princess, becomes suspicious that perhaps this beautiful "foreign princess" is Ash Girl. But unlike her lofty "princess" position of before (when the story begins), this one now includes the father's dawning recognition of his daughter as a beautiful, sexual young woman.

However, full recognition (integration) will take time. On the second night of the ball, Ash Girl again runs away from the prince, this time hiding in her tree—again a retreat to the earlier parental symbols. The image of father coming to chop down the tree with his ax is certainly a fearsome one. The oedipal father is now dangerous and exciting. Her move toward genitality is accompanied by rearoused fears of invasion and damage. Thus one might see this fearsome image of father as both Ash Girl's fear of her father's sexuality and her fear of her own newly discovered sexuality as well. But there is another dimension of father's action: his helping the prince find Ash Girl is an expression of his support for the recognition of her new maturity—his confirmation of her femininity. This important step of integrating genitality into the girl's identity is aided through the relationship with her father. Her erotic longings toward him, and the frustration of these longings, are assimilated into the preexisting, multifaceted relationship with him. Ash Girl's trips to the ball, her retreats, and her father's interventions thus provide a metaphor for the unfolding of this integrative process.

The process finds its resolution in the events of the third day of the festival, with Ash Girl appearing even more magnificent than before. While she quickly runs from the scene so that this time the prince can't follow her, the prince's determination now takes over. Having covered the stairs with pitch to ensnare her golden slipper, he goes straight to Ash Girl's father and announces his intent to marry the slipper's owner. There is at this point a total change in climate: the frightening, ax-wielding (sexual) father now gives way to two different male images, the prince, as Ash Girl's peer, who is determined to find his mate, and a gentler father. First the stepsisters try to squeeze into the slipper. The stepmother's reappearance here brings a striking note to the story: her instructing her two daughters to mutilate their feet in order to claim the prince creates a ghastly image (made palatable by the comic touch of her comment that once they are queen they won't have to walk any more). It may refer both to menstrual blood and to penetration fears, conveying the girl's fears of adult female sexuality. It is also obviously an image of castration, and since this is clearly not the way to achieve success in this story, we would like to think of it as a message in favor of seeing the woman not as a castrated male but as having an intact genital of her own.

All of this is, of course, in stark contrast to the image of purity conveyed by Ash Girl. Once the prince has been set straight about the two stepsisters, he returns to the house-hold and persists, "Haven't you any other daughter?" The father mentions Ash Girl, although he thinks "she can't possibly be the bride" (p. 28). He is not yet fully ready to send her forth, to relinquish her to the prince. But the prince insists. It is now clear that it is not only Ash Girl who longs to go to the ball and all that goes with that: the prince is actively searching as well. No longer frightened or ambiva-lent, Ash Girl comes forth, thrusts her foot forward, and pulls out the other golden slipper. The fitting of the slipper is an ancient folkloric theme and a clear sexual reference. As equals, they find each other. Appropriately matched, they create a safe place for the emergence of genitality. When Cinderella becomes a princess, the king sits with his queen — the resurrected mother, no longer threatening because she is bound in her relationship to the king, and able to admire and accept Cinderella as princess.

Thus the tale of Cinderella (Ash Girl, in the Grimm version) presents us with an interesting series of images. Cinderella does not remain "Cinderella" in the sense in which we have grown accustomed to think of her; rather, she begins as a "princess," loses her status, struggles actively, and, through this struggle, evolves into a princess. She uses her objects in many ways. By the end, we have a triple father image: the actual father, seeming to represent the early father–daughter relationship and its later frightening and exciting sexual dimensions; the prince, who provides an affirmation and acceptance of Cinderella's sexuality; and the king, her new father, representing the affectionate, admiring, desexualized relationship with father. As for the mother: the early bond is disrupted, yet maintained; the envy, rivalry, and prohibitions are actively mastered (for, by the end, the evil stepmother has been deprived of power, her daughters lose the competition for the prince, and they are punished with blindness for their evil ways); the affectionate ties of the good early maternal relationship are maintained so that they can be used for support through individuation and development; and the final identification is consolidated. By the end of the tale, all three — Cinderella and her parents — have their authority and power restored. And Cinderella has achieved her full feminine identity.

POSTSCRIPT

Myths provide us with distillations of the essence of human experience. As a myth, the Cinderella story brings into dramatic focus particular struggles in the girl's evolution toward maturity. Rereading the tale with Doris Bernstein allows us to revisit her ideas about the girl's struggle to separate and individuate from the very mother she seeks to hold on to and identify with; her ideas about the various forms of genital anxiety that must be worked through; her thoughts about the father's role in the daughter's development of her feminine identity; and her understanding of the developing superego and ego ideal. Most important, we share in Doris Bernstein's discovery in Cinderella of the model she had sought for the female oedipal phase. In her study of Electra, she had found a failed oedipal resolution. Here in Cinderella she finds the full resolution, that is, the integration of genitality into the feminine identity. Thus, an interpretive reading of this myth, with its variegated transformation, provides a capsule summary of the components of female identity that we have encountered throughout this volume.

References

Abelin, E. L. (1971). The role of the father. In *Separation-Individuation: Essays in Honor of Margaret S. Mahler,* ed. J. B. McDevitt and C. G. Settlage, pp. 229-252. New York: International Universities Press.

Abraham, K. (1920). Manifestations of the female castration complex. In *Selected Papers,* pp. 338-369. New York: Basic Books.

Aeschylus. *The Libation Bearers.* In *Greek Tragedies,* vol. 2, ed. D. Grene and R. Lattimore, pp. 1-45. Chicago: University of Chicago Press, 1960.

Applegarth, A. (1976). Some observations on work inhibitions in women. *Journal of the American Psychoanalytic Association* 24:251-268.

Barglow, P., and Schaefer, M. (1976). A new female psychology? *Journal of the American Psychoanalytic Association* 24:305-350.

Barnett, M. C. (1966). Vaginal awareness in the infancy and childhood of girls. *Journal of the American Psychoanalytic Association* 24:129-141.

—— (1968). "He won't versus I can't." *Journal of the American Psychoanalytic Association* 3:588-600.

Benedek, T. (1959). Parenthood as a developmental phase. *Journal of the American Psychoanalytic Association* 7:389-417.

Bergman, A. (1982). Considerations about the development of the girl during the separation-individuation process. In *Early Female Development,* ed. D. Mendell, pp. 61–80. New York: Spectrum.

Bergmann, M. (1982). The female Oedipus complex. In *Early Female Development,* ed. D. Mendell, pp. 175–201. New York: Spectrum.

Berliner, B. (1947). On some psychodynamics of masochism. *Psychoanalytic Quarterly* 16:459–471.

Bernstein, D. (1979). Female identity synthesis. In *Career and Motherhood,* ed. A. Roland and B. Harris, pp. 104–123. New York: Human Sciences Press.

_____ (1983). The female superego: a different perspective. *International Journal of Psycho-Analysis* 64:187–201.

_____ (1990). Female genital anxieties, conflicts, and typical mastery modes. *International Journal of Psycho-Analysis* 71:151–165.

_____ (1992). The female Oedipal complex. In *The Personal Myth in Psychoanalytic Theory,* ed. P. Hartocollis and I. Graham, pp. 183–219. New York: International Universities Press.

Blum, H. P. (1976). Masochism, the ego ideal, and the psychology of women. *Journal of the American Psychoanalytic Association* 24:157–191.

Bond, A., Franco, D., and Richards, A. K. (1992). *Dream Portrait: A Study of Nineteen Sequential Dreams as Indicators of Pretermination.* Madison, CT: International Universities Press.

Brooks, G., and Lewis, M. (1979). *Social Cognition and the Acquisition of Self.* New York: Plenum.

Broverman, I. K., Broverman, D. M., Clarkson, F. E., et al. (1970). Sex-role stereotypes and clinical judgments of mental health. *Journal of Consulting and Clinical Psychology* 34:1–7.

Chasseguet-Smirgel, J. (1970). Feminine guilt and the Oedipus complex. In *Female Sexuality: New Psychoanalytic Views,* pp. 94–134. Ann Arbor: University of Michigan Press.

_____ (1984). The femininity of the analyst in professional practice. *International Journal of Psycho-Analysis* 65:169–178.

Chassell, J. (1967). Old wine in new bottles: superego as a structuring of roles. In *Crosscurrents in Psychiatry and Psychoanalysis,* ed. R. W. Gibson, pp. 203–218. Philadelphia: JB Lippincott.

Clower, V. L. (1976). Theoretical implications in current views of masturbation in latency girls. *Journal of the American Psychoanalytic Association* 24:109–125.

Deutsch, H. (1925). The psychology of women in relation to the function of reproduction. *International Journal of Psycho-Analysis* 6:405–418.

_____ (1944). *The Psychology of Women.* Vol. 1. New York: Grune & Stratton.

Devereux, G. (1953). Why Oedipus killed Laius. *International Journal of Psycho-Analysis* 34:132-141.

Dundes, A., ed. (1982). *Cinderella: A Folklore Casebook.* New York: Garland.

Erikson, E. H. (1950). *Childhood and Society.* New York: W. W. Norton.

_____ (1962). Reality and actuality: an address. *Journal of the American Psychoanalytic Association* 10:454-461.

_____ (1964). Reflections on womanhood. *Daedalus* 2:582-606.

Euripides. *Electra.* In *Greek Tragedies,* vol. 2, ed. D. Grene and R. Lattimore, pp. 181-243. Chicago: University of Chicago Press, 1960.

Fast, I. (1979). Developments in gender identity: gender differentiation in girls. *International Journal of Psycho-Analysis* 60:443-453.

Fliegel, Z. O. (1986). Women's development in analytic theory: six decades of controversy. In *Psychoanalysis and Women: Contemporary Reappraisals,* ed. J. Alpert, pp. 3-31. Hillsdale, NJ: Analytic Press.

Forest, T. (1966). Paternal roots of female character development. *Contemporary Psychoanalysis* 3:21-38.

Formanek, R. (1982). On the origins of gender identity. In *Early Female Development,* ed. D. Mendell, pp. 1-24. New York: Spectrum.

Fraiberg, S. (1968). Parallel and divergent patterns in blind and sighted infants. *Psychoanalytic Study of the Child* 23:264-300. New York: International Universities Press.

Frankel, B., and Sherick, I. (1979). Observations of the emerging sexual identity of three and four year old children: with emphasis on female sexual identity. *International Review of Psycho-Analysis* 6:297-309.

Freud, S. (1915). Papers on technique. Observations of transference love. *Standard Edition* 12:157-171.

_____ (1921). Group psychology and the analysis of the ego. *Standard Edition* 18:69-143.

_____ (1923a). The ego and the id. *Standard Edition* 19:3-66.

_____ (1923b). Two encyclopedia articles. (A). Psychoanalysis. *Standard Edition* 18:234-254.

_____ (1924). Dissolution of the Oedipus complex. *Standard Edition* 19:173-179.

_____ (1925). Some psychical consequences of the anatomical distinction between the sexes. *Standard Edition* 19:248-258.

_____ (1926). Inhibitions, symptoms and anxiety. *Standard Edition* 20:77–175.

_____ (1931). Female sexuality. *Standard Edition* 21:223–243.

_____ (1933). Femininity. *Standard Edition* 22:112–135.

Galenson, E., and Roiphe, H. (1976). Some suggested revisions concerning early female development. *Journal of the American Psychoanalytic Association* 24:29–57.

Gilligan, C. (1983). *In a Different Voice.* Cambridge: Harvard University Press.

Glover, L., and Mendell, D. (1982). A suggested developmental sequence for a preoedipal genital phase. In *Early Female Development: Current Psychoanalytic Views,* ed. D. Mendell, pp. 127–174. New York: Spectrum.

Goz, R. (1973). Women patients and women therapists. *International Journal of Psychotherapy* 2:298–319.

Gray, S. W. (1959). Perceived similarity to parents and adjustment. *Journal of Child Development* 30:91–107.

Greenacre, P. (1953). *Trauma, Growth, and Personality.* London: Hogarth.

Greenson, R. (1954). The struggle against identification. *Journal of the American Psychoanalytic Association* 2:200–217.

Grimm, J., and Grimm, W. (1812). Ash Girl (Aschenputtel). In *Cinderella, a Folklore Casebook,* ed. A. Dundes, pp. 22–29. New York: Garland, 1982.

Grossman, W. I., and Stewart, W. A. (1976). Penis envy: from childhood wish to developmental metaphor. *Journal of the American Psychoanalytic Association* 24:193–212.

Grunberger, B. (1964). Outline for a study of narcissism in female sexuality. In *Female Sexuality,* ed. J. Chasseguet-Smirgel, pp. 68–83. Ann Arbor: University of Michigan Press.

Harley, M. (1971). Some reflections on identity problems in prepuberty. In *Separation-Individuation: Essays in Honor of Margaret S. Mahler,* ed. J. B. McDevitt and C. G. Settlage, pp. 385–403. New York: International Universities Press.

Hartmann, H. (1939). *Ego Psychology and the Problem of Adaptation.* New York: International Universities Press, 1958.

_____ (1960). *Psychoanalysis and Moral Values.* New York: International Universities Press.

Helper, M. N. (1955). Instrumental and expressive components in the personalities of women. Unpublished doctoral dissertation.

Horney, K. (1924). On the genesis of the castration-complex in women. *International Journal of Psycho-Analysis* 5:50–65.

Ilg, F. L., and Ames, L. B. (1955). *Child Behavior*. New York: Harper & Row, 1966.

Jacobson, E. (1964). *The Self and the Object World*. New York: International Universities Press.

Jones, E. (1927). Early development of female sexuality. In *Papers on Psychoanalysis*, 5th ed., pp. 438–451. London: Bailliere, Tindall & Cox, 1948.

———— (1947). The genesis of the super-ego. In *Papers on Psychoanalysis*, 5th ed., pp. 145–152. London: Bailliere, Tindall & Cox, 1948.

Kalinich, L. J. (1981). Transference and countertransference in analytic work by and with women. *Bulletin of the Association for Psychoanalytic Medicine* 21:19–30.

Karme, L. (1981). A clinical report of penis envy. *Journal of the American Psychoanalytic Association* 29:427–446.

Keiser, S. (1953). Body ego during orgasm. *Yearbook of Psychoanalysis* 9:146–157.

———— (1958). Disturbances in abstract thinking and body image formation. *Yearbook of Psychoanalysis* 6:628–652.

Kestenberg, J. (1956a). Vicissitudes of female sexuality. *Journal of the American Psychoanalytic Association* 4:453–476.

———— (1956b). On the development of maternal feelings in early childhood. *Psychoanalytic Study of the Child* 11:257–290. New York: International Universities Press.

———— (1968). Outside and inside, male and female. *Journal of the American Psychoanalytic Association* 16:457–520.

———— (1976). Regression and reintegration in pregnancy. *Journal of the American Psychoanalytic Association* 24:213–250.

Kleeman, J. (1976). Freud's views on early female sexuality in the light of direct observations. *Journal of the American Psychoanalytic Association* 24:3–27.

Klein, M. (1945). The Oedipus complex in the light of early anxieties. *International Journal of Psycho-Analysis* 26:11–33.

———— (1975). *Love, Guilt, and Reparation and Other Works 1921–1945*. London: Hogarth.

Lax, R. (1977). The role of internalization in the development of certain aspects of female masochism: ego psychological considerations. *International Journal of Psycho-Analysis* 58:289–300.

Layland, W. R. (1981). In search of a loving father. *International Journal of Psycho-Analysis* 62:215–223.

Leonard, M. (1966). Fathers and daughters. *International Journal of Psycho-Analysis* 47:325–334.

Lerner, H. (1976). Parental mislabelling of female genitals as a determinant of penis envy and learning inhibitions in women. *Journal of the American Psychoanalytic Association* 24:269–283.

Loewald, H. (1979). The waning of the Oedipus complex. *Journal of the American Psychoanalytic Association* 27:751–775.

Lynn, D. (1974). *The Father: His Role in Child Development.* Belmont, CA: Wadsworth.

Mahler, M. S. (1968). *On Human Symbiosis and the Vicissitudes of Individuation.* New York: International Universities Press.

—————— (1974). Symbiosis and individuation: the psychological birth of the human infant. *Psychoanalytic Study of the Child* 29:89–106. New Haven, CT: Yale University Press.

Mahler, M. S., Pine, F., and Bergman, A. (1975). *The Psychological Birth of the Human Infant.* New York: International Universities Press.

McDougall, J. (1986). Eve's reflection: on the homosexual components of female sexuality. In *Between Analyst and Patient,* ed. H. C. Meyers, pp. 213–228. Hillsdale, NJ: Analytic Press.

Menaker, E. (1979). Some inner conflicts of women in a changing society. In *Career and Motherhood,* ed. A. Roland and B. Harris, pp. 87–101. New York: Human Sciences Press.

Mogul, K. M. (1982). Overview: the sex of the therapist. *American Journal of Psychiatry* 139:1–12.

Mohaczy, I. (1983). Psychoanalysis and prevention in childhood mental health. *Contemporary Psychoanalysis* 19:265–275.

Money, J., and Ehrhardt, A. (1972). *Man and Woman, Boy and Girl.* Baltimore, MD: Johns Hopkins University Press.

Montgrain, N. (1983). On the vicissitudes of female sexuality: the difficult path from "anatomical destiny" to psychic representation. *International Journal of Psycho-Analysis* 64:169–186.

Mueller, J. (1932). A contribution to the problem of libidinal development of the genital phase in girls. *International Journal of Psycho-Analysis* 13:361–368.

Nagera, H. (1975). *Female Sexuality and the Oedipus Complex.* New York: Jason Aronson.

Neubauer, P. (1960). The one-parent child and his oedipal development. *Psychoanalytic Study of the Child* 15:286–309. New York: International Universities Press.

Oliner, M. (1982). The anal phase. In *Early Female Development,* ed. D. Mendell, pp. 25–60. New York: Spectrum.

Osgood, C., Suci, G., and Tannenbaum, P. H. (1957). *The Measuring of Meaning.* Chicago: University of Illinois Press.

Parens, H., Pollock, L., Stern, J., and Kramer, S. (1976). On the girl's entry into the Oedipus complex. *Journal of the American Psychoanalytic Association* 24:79–107.

Perrault, C. (1697). Cinderella, or the little glass slipper. In *Cinderella, a Folklore Casebook,* ed. A. Dundes, pp. 14–21. New York: Garland, 1982.

Person, E. (1983). Women in therapy: therapist gender as a variable. *International Review of Psycho-Analysis* 10:193–204.

Reich, A. (1954). Early identifications as archaic elements in the superego. *Journal of the American Psychoanalytic Association* 2:218–238.

Ritvo, S., and Solnit, A. (1960). The relationship of early ego identifications to superego formation. *International Journal of Psycho-Analysis* 41:295–300.

Roiphe, H. (1968). On an early genital phase: with an addendum on genesis. *Psychoanalytic Study of the Child* 23:348–365. New York: International Universities Press.

Ross, J. M. (1979). Fathering: a review of some psychoanalytic contributions on paternity. *International Journal of Psycho-Analysis* 60:317–327.

Sandler, J. (1960). On the concept of superego. *Psychoanalytic Study of the Child* 15:128–162. New York: International Universities Press.

Sandler, J., and Rosenblatt, B. (1962). The concept of the representational world. *Psychoanalytic Study of the Child* 17:128–145. New York: International Universities Press.

Schafer, R. (1960). The loving and beloved superego in Freud's structural theory. *Psychoanalytic Study of the Child* 15:163–188. New York: International Universities Press.

_____ (1968). *Aspects of Internalization.* New York: International Universities Press.

_____ (1974). Problems in Freud's psychology of women. *Journal of the American Psychoanalytic Association* 22:459–485.

_____ (1978). Impotence, frigidity and sexism. In *Language and In-*

sight: The Freud Memorial Lectures, pp. 139–172. New Haven, CT: Yale University Press.

Seidenberg, R., and Papathomopoulos, E. (1962). Daughters who tend the fathers: a literary survey. *Psychoanalytic Study of Society* 2:135–160.

Sheehy, G. (1976). *Passages: Predictable Crises of Adult Life.* New York: E. P. Dutton.

Silverman, L., Lachman, F., and Milrish, R. (1982). *The Search for Oneness.* New York: International Universities Press.

Silverman, M. A. (1981). Cognitive development in female psychology. *Journal of the American Psychoanalytic Association* 29:581–605.

Sophocles. *Electra.* In *Greek Tragedies,* vol. 2, ed. D. Grene and R. Lattimore, pp. 45–111. Chicago: University of Chicago Press, 1960.

Spitz, R. A. (1957). *No and Yes: On the Genesis of Human Communication.* New York: International Universities Press.

Stoller, R. J. (1968). *Sex and Gender: The development of masculinity and femininity,* vol. 1. New York: Jason Aronson.

———— (1976). Primary femininity. *Journal of the American Psychoanalytic Association* 24:59–78.

Torok, M. (1970). The significance of penis envy in women. In *Female Sexuality: New Psychoanalytic Views,* ed. J. Chasseguet-Smirgel, pp. 135–170. Ann Arbor: University of Michigan Press.

Tower, L. (1956). Countertransference. *Journal of the American Psychoanalytic Association* 4:224–255.

Turkel, A. (1976). The impact of feminism on the practice of women. *American Journal of Psychiatry* 36:119–126.

Tyson, P. (1982). A developmental line of gender identity, gender role, and choice of love object. *Journal of the American Psychoanalytic Association* 30:61–86.

Weil, E. (1958). The origin and vicissitudes of the self-image. *Psychoanalysis and the Psychoanalytic Review* 6:3–19.

Witkin, H. A., Dyk, R. B., Faterson, H. F., et al. (1962). *Psychological Differentiation.* New York: Wiley.

Zetzel, E. R. (1970). The doctor–patient relationship in psychiatry. In *The Capacity for Emotional Growth,* pp. 139–155. New York: International Universities Press.

Zilbach, S., Notman, M., Wadelson, C., and Baker-Miller, J. (1979). Reconsideration of aggression and self-esteem in women. Paper presented at International Psychoanalytic Congress, New York, July.

Credits

The editors gratefully acknowledge permission to reprint the following:

Index

DATE DUE